ANXIETY
IN RELATIONSHIP

Free yourself from anxiety and fears, stop suffering and enjoy your love relationship with your partner.

Patricia Peterman

© Copyright 2021 - All rights reserved.

The content contained within this book may not be reproduced, duplicated or transmitted without direct written permission from the author or the publisher.

Under no circumstances will any blame or legal responsibility be held against the publisher, or author, for any damages, reparation, or monetary loss due to the information contained within this book. Either directly or indirectly.

Legal Notice:

This book is copyright protected. This book is only for personal use. You cannot amend, distribute, sell, use, quote or paraphrase any part, or the content within this book, without the consent of the author or publisher.

Disclaimer Notice:

Please note the information contained within this document is for educational and entertainment purposes only. All effort has been executed to present accurate, up to date, and reliable, complete information. No warranties of any kind are declared or implied. Readers acknowledge that the author is not engaging in the rendering of legal, financial, medical or professional advice. The content within this book has been derived from various sources. Please consult a licensed professional before attempting any techniques outlined in this book.

By reading this document, the reader agrees that under no circumstances is the author responsible for any losses, direct or indirect, which are incurred as a result of the use of information contained within this document, including, but not limited to, errors, omissions, or inaccuracies.

Table of Contents

INTRODUCTION 9

CHAPTER 1: ANXIETY IN RELATIONSHIP 13
- PROBABLE CAUSES OF RELATIONSHIP ANXIETY 14
- HOW TO GET RID OF THE ROOT CAUSE? 16
- SIGNS AND HOW TO RECOGNIZE THEM 19
- HOW TO OVERCOME ANXIETY IN RELATIONSHIP 24
- NATURAL WAYS TO REDUCE ANXIETY 28

CHAPTER 2: INSECURITY IN RELATIONSHIP 31
- FEAR OF LOSING SOMEONE 32
- CONSUMING JEALOUSY 32
- PARANOIA AND UNCERTAINTY AS TO WHERE YOUR PARTNER IS 34
- NEED FOR CONSTANT REASSURANCE 34
- HOW TO OVERCOME INSECURITY IN RELATIONSHIP 35

CHAPTER 3: NEGATIVE THINKING AND HOW TO ELIMINATE THEM 39
- BE GRATEFUL FOR EVERYTHING 40
- LAUGH MORE, EVEN WHEN THERE IS NO CAUSE 41
- CHANGE YOUR PERCEPTION AND THINKING ABOUT LIFE 42
- HELP OTHERS 43
- METHODS TO AVOID NEGATIVITY IN THE RELATIONSHIP 43

CHAPTER 4: THE FEAR OF ABANDONMENT 49
- WHY IT HAPPENS 50
- TYPES OF FEAR OF ABANDONMENT 52
- SIGNS OF A FEAR OF ABANDONMENT 54
- THE EFFECT ON RELATIONSHIPS 54
- OVERCOMING FEAR OF ABANDONMENT 57

CHAPTER 5: WHAT IS JEALOUSY? 59
- WHAT ARE THE SYMPTOMS OF JEALOUSY AND HOW TO RECOGNIZE THEM . 62
- TACKLING YOUR JEALOUSY 66
- WHAT'S BEHIND JEALOUSY? 67
- HOW TO OVERCOME JEALOUSY 68

CHAPTER 6: HOW TO OVERCOME JEALOUSY, REGAINING SELF-CONTROL 77
- AVOID CONFUSING FANTASY WITH REALITY 78
- LOOSEN YOUR GRIP 79
- OPEN THE DOOR TO YOUR INSECURITY 80
- LEARN TO TRUST PEOPLE 81

Go to the Root of Your Feelings 81
Put Your Thoughts Black on White 82
Learn From Your Jealousy 82
Get Rid of the "Mental Junk" That Previous Relationships Left You
.... 82
Use Your Energy Better 83
Surround Yourself With People Who Make You Feel Good 83
Meditation as a Method to Manage Your Emotions 84
Don't Judge Others Based on Your Behaviors 84
Don't Fall into the Little Traps of a Relationship 85
Don't Be a Prison Guard 85
Focus on Your Positive Sides 85
Avoid Useless Confrontation With Others 86
Don't Be Afraid of Being Vulnerable 86
Security Always Has a Fence 86
Consult a Therapist 87
Jealousy Does Not Always Bring Doom 87

CHAPTER 7: HOW TO MANAGE YOUR EMOTIONS 91
Stay Committed to Your Daily Mindfulness Ritual 92
Take Up Journaling 93
Work in Harmony with Your Nature 95
Master Your Emotions to Defeat Negativity 97
Importance of Habits in Controlling Your Emotions 99
Self-Regulation Should Work in Concert With Recognizing Your
Emotions 103
Recognizing and Managing Your Emotions 104
Changing Your Emotions 107

CHAPTER 8: SELF-ESTEEM 117

CHAPTER 9: HOW TO SOLVE CONFLICT IN YOUR RELATIONSHIP 121
Why Are We Fighting All the Time? 122
Wait…Are You Saying That Fighting Is Healthy? 128

CHAPTER 10: ACTIONS NEEDED TO OVERCOME THE CONFLICT BETWEEN COUPLES 133

CHAPTER 11: HOW TO MANAGE CONFLICTS 137
Setting the Right Environment 137
Trust 138
Get to the Root of the Issue 138
Pick Your Battles 138
Identify a Middle Ground 139
Limit Yourself to a Single Hurt 139
Don't Build a Hurt Museum 140

DON'T HESITATE TO ENLIST EXTERNAL HELP 140
STAY AWAY FROM NEGATIVITY 140
KNOW WHEN IT IS TIME FOR A TIMEOUT 141
BUILDING TRUST OVER TIME 141
STAYING RESPECTFUL DURING ARGUMENTS 141

CHAPTER 12: HOW TO RESTORE BALANCE IN A RELATIONSHIP 145

FOCUS ON THE PRESENT 145
PERSONALIZE YOUR STATEMENTS WITH "I" 146
AVOID BEING PASSIVE-AGGRESSIVE 146
USE SUITABLE LANGUAGE 147
OPENLY COMMUNICATE YOUR EXPECTATIONS 148
REACH OUT FOR SUPPORT 148

CHAPTER 13: BASIC FOR SUCCESSFUL RELATIONSHIP 149

FORGIVING ONE ANOTHER 150
COMPLIMENTING YOUR PARTNER 151
FOCUSING ON THE POSITIVES 152
UNDERSTANDING EACH OTHER'S DIFFERENCES 152
EXPRESSING INTEREST IN ONE ANOTHER'S LIVES 153
FLIRTING WITH EACH OTHER 153
DON'T FIGHT DIRTY 154

CHAPTER 14: WHY IS IMPORTANT TO ESTABLISH YOUR RELATIONSHIP GOAL 155

TIPS TO KEEP IN MIND 157

CHAPTER 15: EXERCISE TO REDUCE ANXIETY 163

POSITIVE THINKING 163
DISTRACT YOURSELF 163
MINDFUL BREATHING 165
ABDOMINAL BREATHING 166

CHAPTER 16: QUIZ PART: KNOW YOUR LEVEL OF ATTACHMENT AND COMPATIBILITY 169

SELF-ASSESSMENT TO KNOW THE LEVEL OF YOUR ATTACHMENT 169
DECISION MAKING 172
KNOWING YOUR PARTNER 173
THE FUTURE 174
COMPATIBILITY: INDIVIDUAL VERSUS COUPLE TIME 174
COMPATIBILITY: AFFECTION AND SEX 175
COMPATIBILITY: WORK 175
WHAT ABOUT THE EXTENDED FAMILY? 176
WHAT DO YOU CONSIDER YOUR PARTNER TO BE? 177

CONCLUSION 179

Introduction

Relationships are always complicated. Whether you're in one or not, you'll inevitably find yourself wondering about the people you care about and how they're coping. Relationships are complicated. We all know that. And we all know that they can be tricky to navigate. One of the most difficult things about navigating relationships is trying to figure out what someone else is going through. As anxiety tends to accompany depression, it's often hard to tell if you're just depressed, or if you're also anxious. How to deal with that; if you worry about being too open, or not open enough, you can't always tell if someone is truly suffering. Some people don't like to admit their struggles. Some people just don't want to bother you, and others don't want to burden you. It can be hard to tell if your anxiety is a result of something, you're doing wrong, or if your anxiety is a result of something someone else is doing wrong.

How to get information about someone's anxiety?

It's one thing to get a heads up from someone. It's another thing to get all the information you need to understand why your friend is panicking or sad. And it's still another thing to find someone willing to provide all that information to you in a way that is easy to digest. But these tips will help you learn a little bit about people, be sure to be realistic about your relationship. There's a misconception that just because you're interested in someone, you automatically know everything there is to know about them. If you believe that's true, you'll likely do things like getting too close too soon or jump to conclusions without thinking them through first. Instead, be sure to be real and compassionate. Be careful to remember that every person is different.

What to do for someone with anxiety

If you're worried your friend has anxiety, you have a few options:

- **Tell them:** Asking someone who has anxiety, if they have it, can be really difficult and unhelpful. But a simple "Are you okay?" is not a lie, and if they don't like your probing about it, then just let it go.
- **Listen:** Sometimes, it's better to let someone else talk. There are so many facets of a person's mental health that not everyone is comfortable discussing. Just listen and be there for your friend in whatever way you can. Sometimes, it's better to let someone else talk.

Falling and being in love difficulties us from various perspectives. Some of these difficulties are unforeseen, and when we face them the first run-through, our human instinct makes us cautious. For example, if you love somebody without question, and he/she makes you extremely upset, odds are, you will abstain from being helpless. On an individual level, we as a whole dread being harmed, intentionally or unknowingly. Incidentally, this dread will, in general, increment when we are getting what we need. On the off chance that a relationship is acceptable, one begins to fear the 'effect of a separation.' Consequently, he/she begins to take the guard, making the separation, and in the end, cutting off the association. If we are encountering love and being treated in a curiously decent manner, we become tense. That defensive tension becomes a barrier. It is important to note that anxiety in a relationship does not only arise because of the things going on between the two parties involved. This feeling may also occur because of our perception. The items you tell yourself about a relationship, love, attraction, desire, etcetera will affect our lives. This means that you might have the best partner in the world, but your thoughts still hinder you from realizing it and enjoying the moment. The proverbial 'Inner voice' is very dangerous if it is negative. This mental couch can tell us things that fuel our fear of intimacy. The critical inner voice can feed us lousy advice, such as "You are too ugly for him/her," "Even the other people have left you before" "You cannot trust such a man/woman." What do such thoughts do? They make us turn against the people we love and, most importantly, ourselves. The critical inner voice can make us hostile, paranoid, and unnecessarily suspicious. It can also drive our feelings of defensiveness, distrust, anxiety, and jealousy to unhealthy levels. This tiny negative voice feeds us an endless stream of harmful thoughts that make us worried about relationships and undermine our happiness. It prevents us from enjoying life wholesomely.

CHAPTER 1:

Anxiety in Relationship

How are you going to know that you are suffering from relationship anxiety? Are there any definite signs that can determine the various kinds of negative emotions regarding your relationship? How can anxiety affect your relationship? All such questions can be quickly answered when you opt for what is known as self-evaluation of relationship anxiety. The aim of this is to properly evaluate the issue for putting a complete end to it. Anxiety can crop up at any time in relationships. The truth is that every one of us is vulnerable to this necessary kind of problem. You will find that the tendency to get anxious in a healthy relationship will increase as the bond grows stronger. So, everyone needs to opt for self-evaluation. Are you in the habit of spending most of your time worrying about all those things that could go bad in your relationship? A definite sign of relationship anxiety is when you keep worrying as an outcome of all the questions that run in your mind. For the perfect self-evaluation of this definite problem, you will first learn about the signs that will depict whether you are anxious or not. You will also require to assess the effects and causes of the problem you think persists in your relationship. The cause of evaluation is to learn about the problems before they can develop.

Probable Causes of Relationship Anxiety

The majority of the time, relationship anxiety might turn out to be the manifestation of a rooted, deep problem. Some of the most common causes are:

- **Relationship complication:** When the relationship is not defined clearly, or you are not sure about the same, it is classified as being complicated. It can be regarded to all those people who are in the dating stage. For example, a woman might not be clear about a man's motive: whether they are in the relationship just for fun or want to take it to marriage. Even long-distance relationships can lead to relationship anxiety. If this is the case, then both partners are required to trust each other.

- **Continuous fights:** When you just keep on fighting or quarreling with your partner, you will not be able to put an end to your worries. You will always feel tensed or worried as you are unsure when the ensuing fight will crop up. It is a major cause of relationship anxiety. The reason behind this is that your intention of avoiding fights will not let you spend some quality time with your romantic partner.

- **Always comparing:** Comparison of the current relationship with the past ones needs to be avoided. It is not at all a healthy practice. You might breed in feelings of intense regret if you find out that the last relationship was far better regarding communication, intimacy, finance, and various aspects. To keep yourself away from such feelings, never compare your relationship or even marriage regarding others or the ones from your past.

- **Less understanding:** Partners who do not want to invest time to understand one another is bound to suffer from difficulties. As already mentioned above, continuous fights will lead to relationship anxiety. Can you notice the anxiety symptoms along with miscommunications? When understanding is lacking between two partners, relationship anxiety will crop up. Try to invest some time to get to know your partner in a better way. Also, encourage your partner to do the same.

- **Miscellaneous issues**: Tough experiences from your past relationships can lead to other serious issues. Also, neglect or abuse in the past and lack of affection are definite reasons you might suffer from relationship anxiety.

After you have successfully figured out the prime cause of the issues related to your relationship, getting rid of that cause will be the following big step.

How to Get Rid of the Root Cause?

Couples/partners are bound to face various types of challenges which they need to address as they progress. Your capability to manage the issues as they crop up in the relationship will help determine the relationship's growth. In case a challenge or issue is not appropriately managed, you might find your healthy relationship in a phase of the crisis. You might also need to take some serious steps to find your way out of the issue. Some of the most common challenges faced by people in their relationships are relationship needs, communication, developing jointly as a couple, equal rights, contentedness, habit, routine, loyalty, sexuality, fights, stress, value differences, conflicts, illness, distance, and this list will keep going on.

How much care are you and your partner in the relationship? Being considerate and careful can help in avoiding most of the frustrations in your relationship. Are you able to enjoy the moment? Living in the present sounds much more straightforward than doing the same. It might not be now, but sometimes our thoughts from the past or the future will try to slide in. There are certainly other questions that you will need to ask yourself. How much are you enjoying the present moment? Can you make your partner understand what you want to say? Do you both spend a lot of time together doing everyday things? Can you feel tenderness, sexual satisfaction, and security with your partner? Do you find support and peace in the relationship? Can you discuss anything openly with your partner? Do you feel healthy with your partner? As you answer all of these questions, you will guide yourself properly on the road of self-evaluation of various issues that you are facing in the relationship. In most cases, men, in particular, do not like to get indulged in relationship talks. Regardless of that, it is essential to exchange your wishes and needs with your partner regularly. Communication strategies play a vital role, especially in resolving conflicts. First, you will need to distinguish between general communication as partners and communication resulting from conflict resolution.

Communicating about each other's wishes, hopes, plans, and ideas forms a critical foundation block of a relationship. Those couples who are happy for a long time in their relationships can communicate with each other about their feelings. They do not see the relationship or themselves being threatened by all their expressions. It won't even matter if both are negative about their feelings without having an idea. They can develop their gestures, facial expressions, and subtle language throughout their relationship. Fights and quarrels are very typical in a healthy relationship. All that matters are the 'HOW.' Clashes tend to arise whenever you or the other person feels strained by various external stresses. For example, conflicts in the family, problems in raising children, problems in the job, and many others. The partner who feels stressed will communicate with the other person in a more violent or irritated tone.

It is always in your most significant interest to be inventive and proactive about how you communicate with all those who are closest to you. Creating, nurturing, and maintaining relationships with family, friends, and co-workers, not just our partners, is vital for our wellbeing. Instead of just waiting for others to bring in changes in the relationships, the best and the most comfortable place for starting is with yourself.

Signs and How to Recognize Them

Anxiety is a feeling of worry about something you are not sure of or a strong desire to do something. Anxiety can be experienced in various situations. A good example is being anxious when in a relationship. It is where you worry about a particular act in your relationship and what that action will result in. Does anxiety have effects on a relationship? Some of the signs that you are affected by anxiety in the relationship are discussed below:

Lack of Confidence in Your Relationship

Lack of confidence in a relationship is termed as having low self-esteem. It is whereby you feel low, and you are not ready to accept yourself the way you are. Low self-esteem is often caused by non-acceptance by the rest of the world. Most people who are rejected by other people fail to understand that others love and care for them.

A person with low self-esteem will often feel second best in an argument and will not contribute to an argument in a relationship. A high level of anxiety leads to disappointments, and anxious people will seek to deal with perfection, thus ending up having fantasy instead of reality. They will spend most of their time fantasizing instead of building their relationships.

Anxiety Can Raise Suspicion

When one of the partners or friends in a relationship is anxious, they will always suspect the other partner. She will presume that the other partner does not love her or does not give her the required attention.

Anxiety makes one have aggressive behaviors. The other partner in the relationship will take that aggressiveness to try to cheat on them or a sign of the need to end the relationship. Suspicion is very unhealthy in a relationship as it might lead to the end of the relationship. Other vices such as mistrust and conflict arise from suspicion.

Over-Dependence

If you are anxious in a relationship, you will always depend on your partner for support and assurance. You will be worrying about things that are not likely to happen in the future and depend on your partner for assurance. For example, you may be worried about your partner leaving you, which you are not sure of, and always disturb your partner to assure you that he will not leave you. Since you are anxious about rejection, you will keep calling or sending text messages to your partner. If he delays or refuses to pick up your calls or reply to your text messages, you will become anxious.

When you are anxious in a relationship, you will not be able to make independent decisions. You will depend on your partner to make decisions because you think that your decisions are not right. It will negatively affect your relationship because one partner makes all the decisions in that relationship. You will feel like you have your relationship is dominated by one partner, thus bringing misunderstandings in your relationship.

Excessive Anger That Weakens Trust

When you are anxious in a relationship, you will tend to be angry all the time. Anger will negatively affect your relationship as your partner will reduce his trust in you. He might think that you are cheating on him, and you want to end the relationship; that is why you are always angry at him. Anger will create fear in a relationship, especially when the relationship is between a senior and a junior. When you are anxious and angry all the time, the other friend will be afraid and distance himself from you. It will create a negative impact on your relationship because you will not maintain close ties.

Difficulty in Expressing Your Feelings

Anxiety may make it difficult to voice out your feelings. It will impact negatively your relationship. Voicing your truth in a relationship is healthy because your feelings are not suppressed. Sharing your thoughts and how you feel with your partner significantly improves trust. If you are anxious and fail to express how you feel, there will be no trust in your relationship, and intimacy will never thrive. Failing to voice your perception of an issue in a relationship is like a minor in that relationship. You may also fail to express your feelings in an intimate relationship, thus ending up disappointing your partner, who might have had high intentions.

Anxiety Leads to Impatience

When anxious, you can quickly become impatient as things that were previously done easily become hard. Impatience in a relationship is extremely hurtful as it communicates that you do not care about your partner and the relationship. Lack of patience in a relationship weakens the sense of safety, leading to an unhealthy relationship.

When you become worried about things that are likely to happen in the future, you will always be impatient with everyone. For instance, if you are together and he does not act quickly as you want, you will be impatient with him and end up quarreling. You can imagine a relationship where you argue about everything. There will be a complete lack of peace, leading to the end of the relationship.

Anxiety Leads to the Feeling of Insecurity

Anxiety leads to insecurity, whereby you are unsure whether the other person loves you or not, not being sure whether your relationship will last or not can make you give up on that relationship, hence impacting your life. This anxiety feeling can make you feel alone in that relationship, thus creating distance between you and your partner. The main effect of distancing yourself is the feeling of insecurity.

Having Few Relationships

An anxious person will tend to have few relationships because they are always worried about other things. They will not have time for many relationships.

It previously had more relationships; anxiety will end those relationships due to insecurity, anger, mistrust, and impatience. People with anxiety do not have time for other people; they only have time for their worries.

Anxiety Leads to the End of a Relationship

Anxiety causes stress, which will eventually end your relationship. It leads to the rise of other factors such as lack of trust, resentment, low self-esteem, insecurity, concealing of feelings, and avoidance. All these factors will contribute to the ending up of your relationship. An anxious person will become over-dependent and detached from other people and from their emotions too. They may avoid negative emotions such as anger, fear, sadness, and anxiety. He may also be uncomfortable with romantic relationships and end up disappointing their partners. It will lead to the end of the relationship.

Having Difficulty Attending to Other People's Needs

When you are overwhelmed with anxiety, you will be lost in your worries, and you will not have time for others. Not having time for your partner will lead to the suffocation of that relationship. Imagine having a partner who does not have time for you but spends most of his time worrying. Do you think that relationship will still grow? Of course, it will cease to exist when anxiety comes with health effects, such as headache, nausea, shortness of breath, and fatigue. It will mostly see you hospitalized. Therefore, you will not have time for friendship. You will not have time to attend and care for the needs of your partner.

How to Overcome Anxiety in Relationship

Given below are a combination of techniques and strategies to overcome relationship anxiety:

Ask for help

Don't ever believe you need to learn how to manage your anxiety and distress in relationships. Remember how personal therapy can help you handle your relationship and intimacy issues or take steps towards a better dating life. Couple therapy can also help people learn to improve communication in their partnership and develop problem-solving skills.

Develop Your Desires

When you concentrate all of your energy on a romantic relationship, there's a risk you'll feel anxious. People who have good relationships with family and friends who reflect on their personal goals and interests are likely to become better partners and are less likely to experience anxiety or distress, or confusion about the partnership over a breakup.

Examine the Reasoning

Anxiety and depression make it difficult to determine independently whether a question is valid. For instance, if you feel more depressed overall, then you might be persuaded that your spouse would lie or plan to leave you when there is no proof. Think about whether you need to move on to healthy habits to control your distress and anxiety, help connect with your spouse or discuss issues of concern in the relationship.

Share Your Desires

Often people are so focused on making another person like them in relationships that they fail to speak up for their interests and desires. Compromise is part of any relationship, but that doesn't imply that you shouldn't express your thoughts or be assertive when something is important to you. The sooner in a partnership, you will set a precedent for expressing your desires, the less likely you will be to feel resentful.

Don't Avoid

Individuals who feel insecure in a partnership may be inclined to ignore issues that trigger difficulties or protect them from disclosing anxiety-related issues. Avoidance is only a partial remedy, which sometimes results in intense confrontation. Set a norm for grappling with problems head-on in the partnership, even if at first it seems awkward. If you require a third person to help facilitate improved communication, do not hesitate to talk to your partner or meet directly with a psychologist. If you're unsure where to continue, then talk of what you're most worried about when it comes to your romantic partnership. How will your own best version tackle this issue? There is a greater likelihood that you will discover how to strengthen the relationship and handle your anxiety-related issues. Yet there's still support even if you fail. Ask who you should hire now to help you control your insecurity around relationships.

Couple Therapy

It is enticing because you feel for someone by acting as a proxy friend to help them. The issue here is that you are not a psychiatrist. It will be emotionally exhausting to try to perform that part. This could make your partner hate you. You will not have the duty to offer friend counseling.

For this purpose, you should steer your companion kindly into collaborating with a psychiatrist. A psychiatrist may help people change their coping method with fear, inside and outside of a connection.

Remember that couple therapy will become imperative, especially if you're in a serious and long-term relationship. Many of the problems with anxiety may be focused on friendship. Meeting with a relationship psychologist will alleviate your friend from the strain. Rather than telling them to do it yourself, you encourage them to assist her in the counseling.

Accompany Your Partner to Therapy

Irrespective of the fact that your friend supports the offer of going to counseling or rejects it, you can pursue it yourself. It can help you build the skills required to help your partner handle anxiety and distress and deal with it. A psychiatrist will even show you how to treat your stressed spouse more efficiently.

It's quick to think about taking care of yourself while you are meeting with an anxious partner. It will guarantee that you are still focused on your emotional wellbeing by heading to the counseling.

Learn to Communicate About the Anxiety

Anxiety may be terrifying. This will make you even want to not think or talk about it.

Nonetheless, one of the most powerful ways to cope with anxiety and insecurity in a partnership is to address it with your spouse freely, frankly, and personally.

It is essential to have open conversations together about what they know and to confirm those feelings.

If you want to reassure your companion that you embrace their fear, you will allow them to open up about it. Seek to listen without criticizing. Do not get protective or take specific anxiety onto you. You can begin by starting the conversation by asking a question like this: "What do you think I could do to help with your anxiety?"

Natural Ways to Reduce Anxiety

You can make use of several natural ways to reduce anxiety and to help you feel better, including:

Eating A Balanced Diet

A diet rich in vegetables, fruits, good quality meats, seafood, nuts, and whole grains may minimize the likelihood of developing anxiety disorders. Still, diet alone might not be adequate to cure them.

Consume Probiotics and Fermented Foods

Improved mental wellbeing has been linked with taking probiotics and consuming fermented foods.

Reduce Caffeine Intake

Excessive intake of caffeine can worsen anxiety feelings in some people, particularly those with anxiety disorders.

Abstaining from Drinking

Anxiety problems and drug addiction are closely related, and keeping away from alcoholic beverages will benefit.

Stop Smoking

There is an elevated chance of having an anxiety condition. Quitting is related to greater mental wellbeing.

Exercise

Daily activity is correlated with a reduced chance of experiencing an anxiety condition, but evidence remains mixed about how it can benefit people who have already been diagnosed.

Use meditation

One form of meditation-based treatment called mindfulness-based stress management has dramatically reduced symptoms in people with anxiety disorders.

Practice Yoga

Daily yoga exercise has been shown to reduce symptoms in people diagnosed with anxiety disorders. However, further high-quality work is required.

Therefore, eating nutrient-rich food, avoiding psychoactive drugs, and using stress-management strategies will alleviate anxiety symptoms.

CHAPTER 2:

Insecurity in Relationship

In a relationship, both partners will feel loved, valued, and safe. This holy grail of good relationship features is ripped down where there is significant tension in the relationship.

From envy to behavioral influence, insecurity can express itself in several detrimental ways. Your marital insecurity may or may not be rational, but it produces unhealthful conduct irrespective of the rationale. What is significant is that such insecurity can also manifest itself in health issues afterward, as studies have shown. Here are eight symptoms of security in a relationship and what you should do about it.

Fear of Losing Someone

One indication that you are vulnerable in a relationship is a persistent fear of losing a partner. Relationship insecurities make you feel like you're not worth anyone's attention, and you find yourself obsessed as to whether your boyfriend really loves you, really enjoys sex, is drawn to you, finds you irritating, or tries to leave you for anyone else. That concern is all the more understandable after having gone through a tough time with your partner, where they might have lost your trust.

In reality, a set of studies showed that emotional relationship vulnerability was an indicator of sexual frustration. The relationship is lost without confidence. If you're still afraid that you're not going to trust your partner, you shouldn't be together. Trust is the cornerstone of a stable partnership.

Consuming Jealousy

There is a certain degree of envy in a relationship that is considered good. You're in a serious relationship, after all, and you don't want anyone else to ruin what you've set up. Yet there, is a phase when this positive envy is turning into a burning fear. Popular signs of jealousy include:

- Cheating on your partner
- Continuously checking your partner's whereabouts

- Aggression
- Manipulating behavior, such as forcing relationships to stop because they make you insecure
- Being too close or sticking to your partner
- Spite and pettiness, such as having a new friend or flirting with someone else only to make your partner jealous
- Envy is incredibly difficult. That sly feeling is completely reasonable when you're at the moment, but it's not worth sacrificing a decent relationship. Practice how to relinquish any hang-ups and construct trust in a companionship.
- Demanding access to personal electronic devices

One indication that you are insecure in that marriage is your tendency to access your spouse's electronic gadgets, such as mobile phones, laptops, or social media pages. You may be paranoid, wondering if your partner has been engaging in inappropriate conversations online. Hence, you feel you should be keeping her under check, thinking that you're protecting your relationship by doing so.

It feels a bit frightening at first, but to realize that you can't change your partner's behavior by monitoring them like a security officer will give you a sense of peace. At the end of the day, it's either you trust your partner, or you don't.

Paranoia and Uncertainty as to Where Your Partner Is

Continually checking your partner's location and motives can be tiresome for both sides and could undermine your relationship. Sadly, the hardest thing to do when you're insecure is to trust your partner. The soon after you get into an argument with your companion over her true whereabouts, try to tell yourself that if your partner has never given you a reason to question her, you should stop doing so. It is one of the signs of an insecure man in marriage. Insecure husbands tend to exhibit this action rather than wives.

Need for Constant Reassurance

"You love me, huh? Do you really want to be here with me? Are you going to be faithful? Why do you still like me?"

These questions are all motivated by insecurities. If you are unsure about yourself, you may find out that you are constantly requesting your spouse's reassurance for validation.

Unnecessary reassurance-seeking by a spouse is a sign of depression triggered by relationship anxiety. Even though some measure of your partner's reassurance is supposed to make you feel unique about your relationship, it should not dominate your conversations. If you feel stressed or need constant reassurance, therapy can be considered a great way of getting to know yourself better and learning to enjoy who you are.

How to Overcome Insecurity in Relationship

Individuals often enter new relationships with the fears and insecurities that were instilled in them by previous relationships. A relationship can lack the intimacy a person wishes for or may be troubled by suspicion, jealousy, and possessiveness. The reasons behind a person's insecurities will determine how they should be treated to ensure intimacy is maintained through an open and trusting communication process, which is the basis of any successful relationship.

Those who lack confidence in themselves, often worry that their partner is straying or interested in someone else. One common insecurity is a fear of abandonment. This can be attributed to a previous loss of intimacy, or the inability to trust new relationships. Reassurance from a current partner may help overcome these fears, but should only be done so through sincere and honest communication and if the reassurances are genuine. To ensure that a person is not insecure at the beginning of a relationship, they must be sure that they can trust their partner and accept them for who they are; this level of comfort can only be achieved through honest communication. The second stage in overcoming insecurity is to realize that everyone has faults and that these differences add to any relationship rather than undermine it. Realizing that individuals have different personalities can help bring about a sense of acceptance.

Here are 5 Steps to Overcome Insecurities in a Relationship:

- *Step 1: Knowing the root of insecurity. Insecurity is that feeling of being completely exposed and vulnerable.*

Insecurities often stem from a lack of trust and self-love or fear of loss. Understanding the source of your insecurity can help you communicate with your partner about what needs addressing. Honest dialogue is the best way to overcome any relationship issue. And, most importantly, don't forget to be honest with yourself as well...

- *Step 2: Know that you are valued.*

You need to feel your partner's love and commitment when you're insecure. A way to do this is by prioritizing time with your partner and focusing on expressing gratitude. If you still doubt the relationship, make a list of the reasons why you love your partner. Then take some time to read it together during a one-on-one date night or in the morning when waking up next to each other. This is a sure-fire way for your partner to feel your appreciation.

- **Step 3: Practice emotional regulation.**

Avoid criticizing, blaming, or insulting your partner when you're feeling insecure. Instead, talk about your feelings and frustrations compassionately and focus on what you both can do to get over your insecurities. For example, if you believe that your partner is too flirtatious at work, ask them how they'd like to handle the situation so that it doesn't affect both of your reputations at the office.

- **Step 4: Work on building trust.**

Insecurities are often born out of a lack of trust in our partner's feelings for us. If you're struggling with trust, it can help to listen empathetically when your partner shares their feelings with you.

You can also share your feelings with them, ensuring that they know how you feel and how much they mean to you. The simple act of expressing your love will help you feel more secure in the relationship.

- **Step 5: Practice self-love.**

Insecurities can make it difficult to love yourself because they manifest as feelings of insecurity about our ability to be loved by others.

To overcome this obstacle, it's important to remember that you're worthy of being loved and cared for.

To build up self-esteem, practice appreciating your own qualities and take pride in the things that you do well.

CHAPTER 3:

Negative Thinking and How to Eliminate Them

Negativity and positivity are a constant part of life, but negativity has no-so-healthy effects on us and potentially everyone around us. It sets limits on our dreams, goals, and aspirations. Negativity can adversely affect how fulfilling and purposeful our life is. It also has huge effects on our health, whether physical or mental. Studies have shown over and over that people who vibe with negative energy are more prone to stress, anxiety, sickness, and depression than people who are surrounded by positive energy only. When you make up your mind to rid your life of negativity and start encouraging positivity, and you act on this decision, you start to engage in productive things and meet productive people only. Positive experiences sweep away the negative energy in your life.

One thing to know is that you can't completely get rid of negativity because it is a crucial part of life experiences and human survival; however, you can limit the level of negativity you encourage in your life by doing more positive behaviors, thoughts, or actions. Below are tips to help you get rid of negativity and enhance positivity.

Be Grateful for Everything

Entitlement is a dangerous thing because it can make you have skewed expectations of people. It is quite easy to start believing you deserve everything you have when life is all rosy for you.

This could make you develop a sense of entitlement, which causes you to have an unrealistic expectation of others and how they should cater to your needs, wants, and everything else. Selfish entitlement is one of the surest ways to set yourself up for a negativity-filled life.

People who never appreciate the life they have, and live in a constant state of lack and discontentment, so there is no way to live a life of positivity this way. Becoming grateful and showing appreciation for everything you have in life, from the littlest to the biggest, makes you change your mindset from a place of lack to a place of contentment.

Once people notice this new you, it becomes easier to develop harmony in the relationships they share with you. The more grateful you are, the more you receive. This single action can instantaneously make life more positive, fulfilling, and encouraging.

Laugh More, Even When There Is No Cause

Life can sometimes feel draining due to the many activities going on; tight schedules, busy relationships, work, and everything else. Amid all this busyness, it is quite easy to start feeling more like an android rather than a human (no offense to androids). Living with a work-driven, serious mindset will do nothing but bring negative results and performance. It makes you take life so seriously that you forget to laugh sometimes.

Encouraging positivity means living life with a less serious mindset and giving yourself some break. You only live life once, so why burden yourself with all of those responsibilities? Laughter is a great way of reminding yourself that you are human. A laugh brightens your mood and that of people around you; remember, laughter is infectious. Laugh more at jokes and stop being so sensitive to light sarcasm. Too much seriousness will only encourage stress. Do not just laugh at people, though; laugh more at yourself too.

The more you laugh at yourself, and the mistakes you make, the more interesting and exciting life becomes. Happiness is key to positivity, so encourage happiness in your life. Remind yourself of happy experiences in the past and laugh your heart out till you are satisfied. Encourage your brain to release more and more dopamine.

Change Your Perception and Thinking About Life

You have two choices in life; be your friend or be your enemy. To initiate any change in life, you have to start from within yourself. If you want to be rid of negativity and become more positive, change your perception of life, situations, and the circumstances you find yourself in.

A negative perception of life can be corrosive, so start making active efforts to change your perspectives about life. When you fail a test, do not see it as failure or incapability; instead, see it as an opportunity to work harder and do better.

Help Others

Selfishness goes hand-in-hand with negativity, just like entitlement. Stop living for yourself only and start living for others too. This isn't to say you should take on the responsibilities of others and leave yours; it is more about creating a balance between how you help yourself and help others. People who live for themselves tend to have no purpose or calling in life. If you live for yourself and no other person, it would be very hard to live a life of purpose and fulfillment. Negativity defies purpose while positivity accompanies fulfillment and purpose. The best way to start creating purpose in life is to help people around you. Helping people can be something as simple as flashing them a bright smile or asking them how their day went. Doing things for others, no matter how little, gives you a sense of value and direction, which helps you develop positivity.

Methods to Avoid Negativity in The Relationship

Provide Transparent Communication

Good partnerships demand truthful, unrestrained communication; if the individuals in it hold secrets and shut themselves off having actual interactions, no partnership will survive too long.

Relationships will turn bad for the worse easily if people begin disassociating themselves and might not even accept that the other party has done anything or said anything to annoy them.

However, anytime you approach somebody, you will always respond rationally and hold a civilized dialog that doesn't result in shouting and screaming at each other's names. Only note that a good partnership is based on confidence and clear communication, so if you want to prevent conflict, continue to maintain both in each of your personal relationships.

Don't Take Faults from Any Individual

The sure-fire method to launch disagreements and destroy a bond is to quibble up and rub somebody's defects into their face. Know that each individual may have attributes under the surface, but these features do not make up the entirety of whoever they are. Bear in mind, though, that you certainly have characteristics that bothersome, but your near family and friends might not find it a priority to blame you for them. They embrace you exactly the way you are, the faults and all.

If you don't particularly like the company of anyone, you should let the partnership go without tearing down the other individual, just admit the truth to them and reassure them respectfully that somehow you believe it will benefit each of you to head your own way quietly.

Appreciate Each Other

If it's your co-worker, partner, relative, mom, or aunt, let the individual realize that from occasionally, you appreciate them. All in life deserves to be valued, and then they are like they've made a change in the environment. When you accept and compliment somebody's good qualities, they would be motivated to regard you in that very same way. Healthy partnerships require all parties to have affection, commitment, and mutual understanding. Every time you encounter your mate, your co-worker, your partner, and so on, let them realize that you love them and how strongly you really respect them.

Don't Hang onto Grudges in Relation

Everybody makes mistakes, so that doesn't suggest they need to be kept above their heads for their whole life. Agree that occasionally, humans make mistakes, then pardon the individual for the incident. Of course, if someone wanted to harm you deliberately, you would need to handle it a little differently, so most individuals don't go far from their means to inflict other individual's pain. It was actually just an innocent error because, at some stage, no person on Earth would really go through their whole lives without messing up. Know you have made errors in the old days, too, and you might not like anyone to continually reminding you about your failures too.

Quit Jealousy

Everybody in life has a different direction, and some can appear to have success or do better than you would. This doesn't suggest you can equate yourself with them then feel embarrassed simply because everything that you haven't accomplished has been achieved. What about the marathon that your buddy didn't finish?

What about vacations you enjoyed a few years earlier that your friends mentioned you they had dreamed about taking? Don't let envy hit you, for it would deprive you of pleasure and cloud your judgment. Remember all of the great interactions and successes that might not be under the belt that can help put everything in viewpoint and make you happier with others instead of envy them.

Don't Get into The Complaining Trap

Many people see their moments together as an excuse for throwing all their life problems into each other and dissipating their grievances. After the encounter, this leaves all parties feeling exhausted, which uninspired, which opens the way for further conflict in the long term. Speak of ideas, rather than solving issues.

Notice the good stuff of life, and help each other high. Healthy marriages become perfect as all sides become happier, rather than angry.

Do Not Consider Comparing Your Bond to Anyone

Association is special and unique; the bond with your buddy would look completely different than that of the bond with someone else, so enjoy it for what it really is.

If you still desire what you don't have, you can never have healthy relationships, instead of respecting the wonderful interactions, you do have.

Don't Rely on Transformation

Respect people at this instant with whomever they are, instead of pressuring them to adjust for your own gain. People can improve only if they wish to, so please concentrate on what you appreciate about them, rather than blaming them for their mistakes. If they believe you in having to adapt, you may kindly find out a direction for them to better, but don't take this onto yourself to demand that they do.

Kindness Adds to The Partnerships

They would be more likely to demonstrate caring and affection for you if you display concern for the other individual. Be one like what you wish to see in the future, and your partnerships will thrive, and you can draw others with the same passion that you already do.

Laugh

If you have plenty to chuckle about, it's hard to be cynical, so say stories or go for a great weekend with relatives, mates, co-workers, or even your boyfriend.

Do not allow your inner kid to come out to play in the midst of life's seriousness; not only can you become quite light-hearted and happy, but the fun will also put you together and disperse stress.

CHAPTER 4:

The Fear of Abandonment

A fear of abandonment is a psychologically complex phenomenon expected to derive from loss or trauma in children. This apprehension was researched in several ways. Theories behind fears of abandonment include disruption of normal development of young children's social and mental potential, past relationships and experiences of life, and exposure to common norms and ideas. Although it's no official phobia, one of the most common and most destructive fears of all might be the fear of abandonment. Individuals who fear rejection that continue to exhibit compulsive behaviors and thoughts influencing their relationships eventually make them afraid to give up. This fear can be catastrophic. The first thing in overcoming this fear is to acknowledge it.

The main worry that people near you will leave is the fear of being abandoned. Someone may be afraid of giving up. It may be profoundly rooted in a traumatic experience that you have endured as a child or in adult distress. When you fear renunciation, sustaining healthy relationships can be nearly impossible. This paralyzing fear can lead you to the wall to escape harm.

Why It Happens

We are all assumed to be the product of old fears and learned principles in our childhood habits and actions in a current relationship. Many ideas seek to explain the fear of giving up.

An offshoot of Freudian analysis in the theory of object relations, an "object" in one's mind is an individual, a part of an individual, or something which somehow symbolizes one person or another. Item permanence is the idea that this entity doesn't fundamentally alter even though we don't see them. It applies to "the permanence of objects" examined by the psychologist of creation Jean Piaget for the first time. Children know that mum or dad go to work and then come home. He or she doesn't stop loving the kid just because they're apart for a few hours. Meanwhile, the child creates an internal object, which satisfies the children's need for a parent's temporary interaction or psychological image. The accuracy of the item typically develops before age 3. As children grow and mature, the separation times continue and sometimes are created by children when they go to school or stay in a friend's house over the weekend. A child with strong object continuity knows that time apart is not affected by essential relationships. Traumatic events will disrupt the continuity of the object. Death or divorce are common causes, but it may also be affected in circumstances that seem relatively unimportant for the adults. For instance, children with military parents, those with little time for parents, and those with neglectful parents may also be in danger of disrupted object consistency.

Archetypes and Mythology

The mythology is full of stories of abandoned or rejected lovers, particularly women, who only lie behind their whole selves when the lover departs to conquer the world. Every one of us also has a personal story that is not told but is found deep in one's heart. This personal narrative is made up of the layers of our perceptions, which represent the collective unconscious. The fear of giving up is linked from this viewpoint to these universal myths but depends on our recollections.

Prior Experiences

The events of our history trigger many fears. Even if you don't encounter universal theories or archetypes and if your object continuity is intact, you may have been abandoned at some stage in your life. One research showed that our brains tilt immediately before they recall an occurrence and dependent on a sound, scent, or sensation. When we became adults, most of us had a big transition: the death of a loved one, a friend who was gone, a friendship that ended, a transition from high school to college, marriage, and parenthood. Although most of us adjust to changing conditions, somewhere else is not unusual to grieve about what used to be. You may have a high chance of developing this fear if you have undergone sudden traumatic loss, such as losing someone to abuse and tragedy.

Types of Fear of Abandonment

You will be afraid that someone you love will leave physically and will not return. You may be afraid that someone would give up your emotional needs.

You can keep either with your parent, partner, or friend in relationships.

Fear of Emotional Abandonment

It might be less noticeable than abandonment physically, but it's not less painful. Emotional requirements exist for all of us. You may feel unappreciated, unloved, and isolated when these needs are not met. Also, if you are connected to someone physically present, you may feel lonely. You can live in constant fear that it will happen again if, in the past, you have suffered emotional abandonment, particularly as a child.

Fear of Abandonment in Children

The process of separation anxiety is widespread for babies and teenagers. You may scream or refuse to leave if a parent or adult has to leave. At this point, children have trouble understanding when or if the person returns. When they start to know that the beloved comes back, they conquer their fear. It happens on their third birthday for most babies.

Abandonment Anxiety in Relationships

You may believe that in a relationship, you are weak. You may be overly concerned about your relationship and have issues of trust. It could make your partner suspicious. In time, the other individual will escape, perpetuating the cycle of your fears.

Signs of A Fear of Abandonment

Millions battle with terror. Millions. Almost 10% of the population in the US currently has some form of phobia. As far as relationships are concerned, their resulting habits include being quick to meet, or even to inaccessible partners or friends; you are unwilling to commit entirely and have had very few long-term relationships. The study showed a rise in the readiness of unwanted sex for certain women, while in a relationship, you stay irrespective of how good the relationship is. You're always difficult to please and nitpicky, intimacy with yourself is awkward, you're dangerous and unspeakable of affection, and you find it difficult to trust others.

The Effect on Relationships

There is a unique fear of abandonment. Many of us worry that a romantic partner will be lost.

Some worry that they are suddenly entirely alone. An example of how a regular partnership can begin and develop is to understand how individuals who are afraid of rejection can communicate. It is particularly valid for romantic connections, but even in close friendships, there are several similarities.

The Getting-to-Know-One-Another Phase

You feel very secure at this stage. You are still not emotionally interested in the other person, and you can continue to live your life with your chosen person.

The Honeymoon Phase

It is the phase when you want to commit. You're ready, because you get along so well, to ignore potential red or yellow flags. You start spending a lot of time with the other guy, always enjoy yourself t and feel comfortable.

The Real Relationship

The honeymoon period cannot last forever. Regardless of how beautiful two people are, true-life still needs to happen. It takes time to do things. People get ill, have family issues, start working long hours, and worry about money. Although this is a very natural and optimistic step in a relationship, it can be frightening if you fear that the other person will leave. If you're afraid of that, you probably struggle and make a considerable effort not to voice your thoughts for fear of clinging to it.

The Slight

You are a human being; you have defects in your personality, moods, and things. Regardless of how much you care about other people, you can and should not expect that person to be at the forefront of your mind. An obvious mild thing will inevitably happen, mainly when the honeymoon period is over. It also takes the form of a message with a reply, a phone call without a response, or a request alone for a couple of days.

The Reaction

It is a turning point for those who are afraid of abandonment. If you are afraid of this, you probably completely understand that your partner does not love you anymore. Is it the fear of loss, its severity, and the patient's preferred coping style almost absolutely decided? Some people handle this, insisting that their partner displays love by jumping through a hoop, by being sticky and demanding. However, others believe that the minor is their fault and seek to become the "complete mate" to keep the other person out. The weakness is probably not at all small. Simply put, people often do things their partners don't know. The partner should understand the situation in a stable relationship for what it is, a natural reaction that has little to nothing to it.

Or he may be angry, but either discuss it calmly or discuss it briefly. Nevertheless, a person slightly perceived does not overpower the feelings of the partner.

Overcoming Fear of Abandonment

After you realize your fear of giving up, you can do some things to start healing. Stop the harsh self-judgment and take a relaxed approach. Remember all the positive features that make you the right partner and friend. Discuss your fear of abandonment with the other person and how it came to be. However, be mindful of what you deserve from others. Explain where you are from, but don't make something for them to fix your fear of abandonment. Don't expect more than fair from them. Work on friendship maintenance and develop your network of support. Substantial medications can strengthen your sense of belonging and self-worth. Consider talking to a qualified therapist if you find this unmanageable. You may take advantage of individual advice. When your anxiety is moderate and well-controlled, you could only think about your patterns and learn new behavioral techniques. However, most people's fear of abandonment is due to deep-seated problems that are hard to solve. Professional support is also required to resolve this anxiety and develop the trust needed to improve your thoughts and actions truly. While it is essential to handle fear itself, it is also necessary a sense of belonging. Reflect on creating a community instead of focusing all your time and attention on a single partner.

Nobody can solve all our problems or fulfill all our needs. But each of us can play a significant role in life for a large group of many close friends.

CHAPTER 5:

What Is Jealousy?

Jealousy is a strong feeling of envy or desire to possess something or someone. It can also be an emotion felt when someone takes or is about to take, what he/she feels rightful belongs to him or her. In fact, jealousy is one of the most human of all emotions. Why? Because it is the fear of losing something you have or someone you love, to someone else.

There are many types of jealousy:

The first type is possessive. This occurs when someone feels a strong desire to possess someone. It's usually associated with romantic love and sexual attraction.

The second type is emotional. This happens when you feel that your emotions or affection are threatened by another person or persons that may come in between your emotions for another person you care about. This typically happens in friendships, sibling relationships, parent/child relationships, and a multitude of other interactions. It comes in many forms: fear of abandonment, fear of ridicule or embarrassment by the person you care about most, the risk of losing trust and confidence that you have worked so hard to earn with that person. If someone breaks into your close circle of friends it can be troublesome to maintain a friendship with all parties involved.

The third type is situational. This happens when you feel that your "territory" is being threatened by someone or something. This can be when a spouse is not sticking to the budget and spending too much money out of the family account when a friend is spending too much time with his/her friends instead of with you; it's even experienced by parents when their children become self-sufficient and "leave the nest." We also experience situational jealousy in our jobs. When someone close to us gets a promotion or is offered a job in another city. We can become territorial of our relationship with that person when they are no longer available to us physically because they are too far away from us.

Jealousy can be caused by many things and can affect anyone in many different situations. People who experience these strong feelings should examine their feelings to determine the cause and try to work through it.

You should also keep in mind that once the threat has passed, it's best to forgive and forget. While holding a grudge will not help you get the desired results from the other person, it is hard to forgive some people, and you must try. Jealousy can be a very destructive emotion if not dealt with properly.

Jealousy in a new relationship can be expressed in many different ways, and if not handled well, this emotion can ruin your personal relationships. It is important to understand it and know how to handle it properly. We should know when we are jealous, why we are jealous, and what to do about it. It can be an indicator that something is wrong in the relationship or in your life.

It is a feeling of mistrust, fear, anxiety, and/or anger directed at a rival (real or perceived) over the desired item, value, or relationship.

What Are the Symptoms of Jealousy and How to Recognize them

When you experience it, it has been shown that your emotions cause you to become somewhat mentally unstable. You may start to feel worthless. This can cause you to do unreasonable things. Thus, it is crucial to know the signs and symptoms and determine if you are experiencing them. This way, you can avoid acting in the form of saying things that you may regret later on down the line. You can inoculate yourself from the worst aspects of this type of behavior by merely staying vigilant to the signs that you are heading down this path. Keep in mind that you are a person worthy of love and affection. There is no need for you to be jealous of anybody. A romantic relationship cannot survive chronic jealousy. You have to know the difference between out-of-control envy and healthy concern. The following are the most common signs that you are taking things too far:

Constant "Checking Up"

If your partner does not know where you are, he/she might call you as they are simply concerned for your safety and security. This kind of behavior is healthy and normal. However, when your partner checks on you regularly by texting or calling every hour of every day, they may be exhibiting unhealthy and jealous behavior. Your partner may be feeling insecure. Bear in mind that healthy couples in well-functioning relationships do not feel the need to check up on their partners continually. They feel secure in their relationships and retain trust at all times.

Looking Through Phones and Other Personal Belongings

If you are in a healthy romantic relationship, then there is no need for you to look through the personal belongings of your partner, such as his/her phone or social media accounts. You trust the person, so you do not believe that he/she will cheat on you or leave you.

If you are committed and happy, there is no fear of infidelity. On the other hand, if you are incredibly insecure or jealous, you may look through your partner's stuff for evidence of cheating.

Constant Accusations

If you are in a loving relationship, you will not feel the need to flirt with anyone else.

You and your partner both feel this way. However, if you are in an unhealthy relationship, you may regularly accuse your partner of flirting or cheating. You do not feel secure, and your jealousy drives you to have irrational thoughts and make unreasonable claims.

Never Letting Your Partner Do Anything Without You

If you are jealousy in a relationship, you will start acting possessive. You will try to find out what your partner is up to and find a way of putting yourself into their plans. There's nothing wrong with wanting to get involved in what your significant other is doing, but it reaches a point and becomes tiring. Remember that healthy relationships require a decent amount of space. It's okay to let your partner go out and lose themselves a bit so that they may come back to you feeling refreshed and with a higher capacity to love you. But if you tend to force your way into whatever your significant other is doing, they might eventually come to resent you, for being an unrelenting distraction

You Avoid Facing Issues Affecting Both of You

The main reason why jealousy people avoid issues that involve their partners is that they are afraid that they might upset them and consequently lose them. On the contrary, not facing the problems that are troubling your relationship is more likely to cause a rift than addressing the issues. For instance, the insecure person might not be comfortable with the way their partner oversteps their boundaries, always butting in and distracting them when they are unwelcome. Still, they are afraid of raising this issue, thinking that their partner will become mad about it and possibly even want to leave, which would be catastrophic.

Being Obsessed with Their Exes

There's nothing wrong with being curious a little and wanting to know what kinds of people your partner dated in the past and how it turned out. But if you are obsessed with the people that your partner went out with in the past, it might be stemming out from your insecurities, wanting to measure up to them. If you find out they were better than you, it makes you feel bad, but if you consider yourself better than them, it makes you happy. Insecure people tend to ask their partners to give away details of their past relationships in hopes that they will be considered the best partner yet, to boost their fragile egos.

Controlling Their Partner

A jealous person feels threatened, and in response to that hideous feeling, they want to control their partner. They start to watch their every move, ever ready to read malice and then offering alternatives. For instance, they might begin to screen their partners' friends, and then ask their partner to get away from certain people. When they do this, they fail to acknowledge the fact that their partner had a life before they ever met, and it would be insulting to suggest that he get rid of certain people from his life despite their history together. If the insecure partner doesn't have the power to influence their partner directly, they will start using indirect means, such as doing something that their partner doesn't approve of, to bully them into bending into their will.

Constant Need for Reassurance

A jealous person will seek constant reassurance from their partner. They will want to be reassured that they are still loved, still appreciated, even desirable, yet funny. But it almost seems like they don't believe it because they will always counter their partner's assertion. For instance, the insecure might ask, "do you love me?" upon which their partner replies, "of course I do!" but then the anxious person will say, "if you love me, why didn't you announce on Facebook yesterday that it was our fifth anniversary?" an insecure person will always have a counter-argument, and such behavior escalates the conflict.

Tackling Your Jealousy

If you are struggling in your relationship with jealousy, you may want to think about why you feel jealous. For instance, do you struggle with self-esteem, or do you fear that your partner will leave you? Or, in the past, has your partner been unfaithful, and you're worried that it's going to happen again?

- Accepting that your jealousy hurts your marriage.
- Confess that you are jealous.

- Agree that your spouse is not spied on.
- Discuss the origins of your jealous sentiments.
- Decide to change your conduct.
- Realize that someone else cannot control you, but you can control your response.
- If necessary, seek professional assistance as a couple.
- Set fairground regulations that both of you can agree to.

It is difficult to deal with and can destroy relationships and create toxic marriages when jealousy becomes unhealthy. For this reason, if you experience overwhelming jealousy that interferes with the health of the marriage, finding a neutral party is important to help you understand why there is jealousy. Healthily, this person can give you tools to cope with jealousy.

What's Behind Jealousy?

Underlying jealousy is the fear of loss and abandonment. Often the jealous partner fears that the relationship will end, fears of losing self-esteem or losing "face" with their friends. It is fear that creates feelings of insecurity.

When fear subsides, so does jealousy. On the other hand, the more the feelings of fear increase, the more jealousy generates anger, hatred for love "rivals," disgust (sometimes for themselves), and despair.

So, why should a person be jealous?

An example: The ex-wife cheated on you, and that created ghosts in you. Of course, if your partner has sexual intercourse with other people, then jealousy is absolutely justified. And maybe the whole relationship should be reevaluated. But in this case, one feels excessively jealous without real evidence that refers to a partner's incorrectness or infidelity. First of all, recognize your jealousy.

How to Overcome Jealousy

The first step to overcoming it is accepting that it exists in the first place. It isn't surprising that many people cannot even admit that they have jealous feelings. They can't even admit it to themselves, which is an issue. You know the signs you experience, the anger and unrest you get whenever you feel your relationship is threatened. You know that you have these seemingly exhausting jealous feelings, so you must confront these emotions.

Factors You Should Accept About Jealousy

Accepting that you are jealous is a fact. There are other facts that you need to accept as well before you can begin working on it.

Jealousy won't disappear overnight: Do not make the false assumption that your jealous feelings will suddenly dissipate into thin air. Recognize that it is present, and you need to learn how to deal with it without allowing it to take over your beautiful life and relationship. This is a feeling that has probably resulted from an underlying problem with your confidence or self-security. Realize that it might take some time for you to learn how to deal with this feeling. You might have to do a lot of work on yourself before you will finally begin to feel in control of your emotions again.

You have to confide in your partner about your jealousy: Remember that the object of this feeling is your partner, and they are probably not comfortable with the signs of jealousy they see in you. They might have even tried to reassure you that you have them all to yourself. But it still doesn't diminish these jealous feelings. So, why not talk to them about your feelings instead of expressing anger or frustrations or blaming them for something that might be in your head? Remember that you love this person. So, have that talk with them where you refrain from putting any blame on them but try to be as open as possible. You can say something like "I have these jealous feelings whenever I see you chatting with _____. I know I shouldn't feel this way, but I can't seem to help it. I will love for you to help me with dealing with these feelings." An understanding partner should be able to treat the issue as if it was another challenge the relationship was facing and not leave their partner to sort things out all by themselves. You and your partner now need to accept there is an issue that needs to be resolved. Hopefully, with your partner's full support, you can begin to take positive steps towards working on it.

Step 1: First, Identify the Cause of Your Jealousy

It doesn't act on a person like that, and by now, you should understand that your partner may be the object of your jealousy, not the reason. Something they do or say can indeed trigger it, but you can't blame them for these feelings if you genuinely want to overcome them. The reason has to do with you fundamentally, and it is time to determine the cause. I have to put together a few important questions you can answer. Hopefully, your honest answers will lead you to pinpoint the exact cause of your jealous feelings towards your partner. These questions have been divided into different categories according to what I have found out to be the leading causes of jealousy.

Step 2: Acknowledge Your Jealousy

If you have been able to identify what's causing your jealousy (i.e., insecurities, low self-esteem, fear, or doubt), then that's great! We can now move on to the next step. If you are still unsure where the jealousy arises, then hopefully, after this stage, you should have got it right. Then you can properly learn to deal with these feelings. Here we will look at acknowledging it in an efficient and workable way, through writing.

Experts in psychology have over the years used this method of writing about feelings like anger, worry, pain, and forgiveness to help individuals confront their thoughts and emotions so they can face them properly. It is also a way of positively motivating yourself and feeding your mind with the kind of feelings you want to have or the kind of person that you want to be. For example, a person that believes they are not good-looking can write down somewhere visible in a positive way they would instead look at themselves.

Writing down statements like "I am beautiful inside and out," "I am an attractive man/woman," and "I am a unique person" and reading it to yourself every day can help gradually build up your low self-esteem and become more confident. This approach can also work for jealousy if you can honestly write about your feelings. It will reveal to you the extent to which this is affecting your relationship. So, get a writing pad and paper (or whatever works for you) and get started.

Step 3: Turn Your Jealousy to Pride

"Jealousy is not you, and you are not jealous," says Robert Leahy of the book: "The Jealousy Cure." He also explains that you can view it like a breath of air, which we inhale and exhale without even paying attention to it. This means that it can be something that enters and leaves our minds. The problem arises when it remains in our thoughts and starts to gain control. This should be viewed as an emotion, which can come and go, like anger or hurt. You can't continue to feel angry all the time, can you? It goes away eventually, and so can jealousy.

Let us look at how to channel it into a more positive feeling like pride. Pride in this sense means instead of feeling all the anger and resentment towards your partner, you begin to see the good about them, and you are proud of them and your relationship. Pride here also means countering your jealous thoughts with more positive energy and feeling.

Here are some more pointers on how to turn it into pride:

Be confident in yourself all the time: Enough can never be said of how the lack of, or low self-confidence, brings about jealousy. So, become confident. Believe that you are enough for your partner and that they understand. Remind yourself of the great features that you possess and why your partner is lucky to be with you. If you don't blow your trumpet, who will? So, tell yourself over and over again. "I am handsome/beautiful, funny, hard-working, and a great partner." Simply put, love yourself! If it helps, then write these positive statements down to remind yourself and tell yourself every time you find that you are caught up in jealous thoughts. Invest in reading motivational books that can boost your confidence if you find this helpful. It is unlikely jealousy can dwell in your mind for a long time if you are confident in yourself.

Stop comparing yourself to others: Remember that everyone is unique in their way, so please stop comparing yourself to that guy/lady your partner might be chatting with. No one can be you, so believe in yourself. Comparisons can create envy and jealousy. No need to state this again, be proud of yourself. And when jealous thoughts begin, and you think, "It's because I don't drive the kind of car that he does," "I am not as pretty as she is, counter those thoughts with "His car is great, and my car is good enough for me now, I worked hard to get it," "I am an intelligent and attractive woman."

Believe in your partner: Have some faith in the partner you have chosen. Believe in them and decide to trust and be proud of them all the time. Let your partner know that you are pleased and confident in them even though you can see the threats all around. It helps them to respect and be proud of you as well because of the level of maturity and security you are showing instead of jealousy.

Step 4: Ignore the Competition

"They are not your competition if you don't even compete," says an anonymous writer. There is no open competition except that we create. A lot of jealousy is fundamentally derived from comparing ourselves or relationships with others. We think, "Why is that guy always trying to talk to my partner? Does he think he is better than me?" "He has a better job than me. Maybe that's what she sees in him," "Maybe if I were as slim as she was, he would pay me more attention." A lot of these thoughts go through our heads and create jealous feelings. But really, why the comparison?

There is indeed a fundamental part of our primitive nature that wants to compete. This is like the animals we see in the jungle that compete for almost everything, including food, territory, and mates. But we are not the animals in the jungle, and we have higher and more advanced capabilities to control some of these instincts. We are unique in ourselves, and rather than comparing and letting jealousy take a better part of us. We can focus on our relationships and ourselves. We can continue to add value to ourselves and do what we want to do, not because of the influence of any competition.

Step 5: Handle Awkward Situations like A Pro

People wonder how to handle awkward situations with their partners without getting jealous. For example, how do you handle other men talking to your female partner when you are right there watching and probably waiting? How do you handle others dancing with your partner? Giving them hugs, kisses, perhaps? Does that stir up jealousy in you? Some of these situations can be daunting, almost like a temptation calling out for you to get upset or fight with your partner. But there is always the right way to handle things without exploding in a rage of jealousy and doing any havoc to your relationship.

CHAPTER 6:

How to Overcome Jealousy, Regaining Self-Control

It may sound trivial, but how about starting to believe your partner?

Sometimes you may be wary of your partner, but it is essential to find the strength to act as if you believe him. If you've got to make sure it was really there where he said he was, stop to do it and begin to give in to feelings that manifest to you.

We should avoid asking ourselves why someone loves us. Whether they love you is due to an indefinable quality that you possess and cannot be explained. So, stop trying to "understand" why you may like it.

But people are not objects or toys that must be constantly supervised. If you want to love someone correctly, you have to be willing to lose them. Anger, fear, and jealousy drive away from the love that needs a bit of courage to grow. You may be afraid of losing your loved one (and perhaps you often fear how it will feel afterward), but if you really want to use your imagination, think about the "worst" that could happen, and you will feel better.

Try writing 10 positive ways you will rebuild your new life if your relationship ends. Imagine how you could live without your partner.

Fear is certainly stronger when we feel we have no other options, so avoid basing our entire life on one person.

Avoid Confusing Fantasy With Reality

Jealousy often stems from a destructive use of fantasy. So, avoid listening too much to your imagination.

Think about it: Your partner comes home later than you thought. So, you begin to imagine that he had an aperitif with that "beautiful" person who works in his office or with that other very sensual person that you happened to see in passing in the gym.

You get angry, upset, scared—but you have no proof that what you imagined is real.

As soon as he comes home, you react in a "strange" way, very coldly or, on the contrary, you get angry and lose control. Your partner, in turn, gets defensive and angry.

When you feel very angry, try to throw your thoughts out already, detailing what you imagine your partner is doing while they are out without you. It will help you rationalize.

When you stop being emotional just because you've imagined something, takes a step forward and try to regain control of jealousy.

Loosen Your Grip

Keeping him "imprisoned" will only serve to build the desire to escape your possessiveness. Let it go free (which doesn't mean that you put your feet on your head). If you're dating, let them talk to the attractive co-worker (be aware that they may find their co-worker less attractive than you imagine). If you suspect he wants to make you jealous, short him out by being relaxed.

Imagine your partner out with someone else? See them talking and laughing with someone else?

If you really can't turn off the alarm, it can help concentrate jealousy thoughts at a time slot of the day. It will help you learn not to give in to the impulse to postpone it to 1 hour of your choosing. Jealousy can ruin even the most solid and well-established relationships. It can be a powerful sign that it's time for you to change something in your romantic relationship. Jealousy can be an excellent indicator to understand your underlying feelings better to take the necessary action to protect your relationship from disastrous situations. Here are some methodologies to help you manage jealousy and insecurity within a relationship:

- Questioned every time.
- Whenever you feel even remotely jealous, investigate the feeling underlying the perception of jealousy.
- Is jealousy a consequence of my anger, of ever anxiety, or of my fear?
- What is it that makes me jealous?

When you put the feeling haunting you under the magnifying glass, you take small steps to transform a negative perception into a positive one.

Open the Door to Your Insecurity

Staying available to discuss with your partner what makes you insecure will reinforce a channel of communication that can make a romantic relationship truly solid. Rather than letting yourself be carried away by your jealousy and saying inappropriate things to your partner, share with them what is bothering you. You can say, "the relationship and the way you behave with X make me insecure about our relationship…"

Together, if both of you are interested in being together, you may find ways to get through this moment.

Learn to Trust People

Get into the habit of knowingly trusting people unless you have hard evidence to doubt. Stalking and chases can create a dangerous relationship climate and maybe ruin a relationship for no reason.

Go to the Root of Your Feelings

It is not easy to understand the nature of your pangs of jealousy.

Why do they appear every time someone compliments your partner?

It often becomes irrepressible to blame the partner for their uncontrolled emotions. However, having the courage to dig into your feelings can prove to be the only way to go.

See what you feel with more compassion and objectivity. Reflect on the consequences that your visceral insecurity can lead to.

Why are you always the jealous one between the two?

Is it because you don't want to lose it?

Is it because your previous relationship ended in cheating?

Are you overwhelmed by the belief, even unconscious, that your partner must belong exclusively to you?

Are you pervaded by a visceral sense of inadequacy that does not allow you to live a romantic relationship safely?

Once you have identified the roots of what you are feeling, it will be easier to find a way out to manage an attack of jealousy better.

Put Your Thoughts Black on White

Writing down what you feel and feel on paper will help you uncover certain events, circumstances, and facets that can explain a whole range of your irrational behaviors. Once you have identified the underlying feelings behind jealousy, it will be much easier to manage it.

Learn From Your Jealousy

You can draw many valuable lessons from your jealousy. For example, if your partner knows how to play the guitar so well that he often becomes the center of attention in the evenings, you may start to let him give you lessons instead of living it badly. You would turn something negative into positive.

Get Rid of the "Mental Junk" That Previous Relationships Left You

One of the reasons why you constantly feel the danger that your partner may cheat on you can originate from your previous relationship. Maybe your ex cheated on you with your best friend. You may have been impacted so strongly that you see the very nature of a romantic relationship in a strongly negative light.

Use Your Energy Better

Instead of becoming entangled in the obsession that your partner is lying to you, try to focus your energies on your interests outside the relationship itself. Don't make your partner the only focus of your existence, even if it means a lot to you.

Cultivate your hobbies, hang out with your usual friends, volunteer, learn a foreign language, sign up for a dance class. Anything that will distract your attention from jealousy will give you unexpected energy.

Surround Yourself With People Who Make You Feel Good

Sometimes you immerse yourself completely in your relationship to forget all the other people you have shared your existence with. We are convinced of the importance of spending every single minute with our partner. It is a dangerous approach because it exposes us to total loneliness if the relationship begins to have some problems. And so, we fall into insecurity and despair.

Meditation as a Method to Manage Your Emotions

Meditation is a great way to calm the nerves and manage the flow of emotions. Get used to tuning into your physical and mental self by identifying your thoughts and feelings through deep breaths.

Try to detach yourself from negative emotions such as insecurity and jealousy. Find a quiet corner, free from the usual distractions. Sit comfortably and start eliminating all thoughts by breathing deeply.

Don't Judge Others Based on Your Behaviors

We perceive others based on who we are as if others are a reflection of ourselves. Don't use your behaviors as a yardstick to gauge your partner's.

Recognize a problem and talk to a therapist about it instead of dumping your mental frustrations on your partner.

It is often impossible to understand why our partner, despite the evident absence of concrete elements, continues to make us the object of attacks and unfounded accusations. These are situations in which the problem is not ours but hers.

Don't Fall into the Little Traps of a Relationship

It is often thought that being jealous is a way to make your partner feel important. Don't fall into this trap. Being too jealous will encourage your partner to engage in certain behaviors. It will demean you in their eyes, and it won't make you feel good.

Don't Be a Prison Guard

Go in search of serenity and let go of that desire to lock your partner in prison. The more you try to do it, the more you reinforce his urge to escape. Give him the space to hang out with his friends and all those things that, up to now, you have experienced as a threat. Show yourself confident in who you are and what you want, and, in their eyes, you will remain attractive and irresistible.

Focus on Your Positive Sides

Each of us has virtues. In the depths of our soul, there is a "treasure room." The goal of your life should be to find the way to get there. Once there, being well and feeling safe will be natural because you will perceive your worth beyond whatever behavior those around you assume. If you know you are worth it, you know you deserve love... and you discover that no one, after all, can harm you without your permission.

Avoid Useless Confrontation With Others

Jealousy, as we have said, is often the mask of low self-esteem. When you are convinced that you are not worth it, that you are not good enough or beautiful enough, you open yourself to the abyss of insecurity.

Don't Be Afraid of Being Vulnerable

Life teaches us this whenever it can: there is no real gain without risk. A relationship can give you a lot, but only if you are ready to take the risk of losing everything. It is a risk to share your feelings. It's like giving the keys to your safe to someone else with the promise that it will add value to your treasure. But running the risk of taking everything away.

Security Always Has a Fence

Try to think that you are a prehistoric man in the middle of the open sea; no knowledge of where you are, no map that gives you the perception that there is a land to tread on somewhere. Being scared would be more than understandable. It is a human need that we have been carrying on since the dawn of time: we need borders to feel safe. Our psyche is no exception. It needs borders, not limits.

We need a safe space so that we can then venture into new spaces and set wider boundaries.

What are the boundaries in a relationship? They must be established at the beginning: How far is "flirting" with someone else accepted? What about a kiss on the cheek? And dance with someone of the opposite sex?

Once common ground is established, it will be easier to define the "who," "how," and "when" one is betraying the agreements made together. Border security has always been the basis of good neighborly rules.

Consult a Therapist

If you are struggling with obsessive and extreme jealousy that you cannot manage with self-development strategies, you should speak to an experienced psychologist for a professional solution. Excessive jealousy can manifest itself in different ways within a relationship: physical violence, angry verbal attacks, constantly unstable behaviors such as paranoia, anxiety, *etc*. Working with a therapist will help you take concrete steps to overcome jealousy and the underlying problems that trigger it.

Jealousy Does Not Always Bring Doom

After getting confused in your head about the need to keep jealousy at bay to keep a relationship healthy, what I will tell you below may seem a bit contradictory… but I assure you it is not.

Jealousy, in small sips, can turn out to be an elixir to improve oneself and consequently energize a relationship. The difference will be made by distinguishing "protective" jealousy from "destructive" jealousy in a relationship.

Does your partner express admiration for someone's physicality? It might be time to hit a gym and get fit. Is your partner blown away by the speaking ability of a conference speaker? How about taking a diction course and buying a thesaurus?

The question of a lifetime is: how should I use the stimuli that reach me from the outside? A question that hides the great secret of the alchemists: to find a way to transform lead into gold. After all, it is the true mission of our existence: to illuminate our dark rooms, those that have taught us not to open from an early age.

We must find out who we are, and we can only do it by having the courage to face the unknown that lives in us.

You'll be alert even in your rest to see even the most straightforward sign of loss or abandonment. Subsequently, the restless evenings, frequented by the adversary: jealousy, enthralled by the connection jail once more.

Jealousy relationships can be an executioner for any couple. If you're jealous, your lover will feel like you don't trust them. Being jealous is anything but difficult, and sometimes it feels like a natural response. However, you should attempt to expel jealousy from any relationship.

Not all individuals have a problem with a jealous partner. It appears odd that an individual would need to aggravate and upset their partner. Yet, it happens regularly in jealousy relationships since certain individuals feel that if they can make an individual jealous, the other individual cares about them more. That, obviously, isn't reality.

CHAPTER 7:

How To Manage Your Emotions

To truly master your emotions, you will need to go a lot further than just engaging in sporadic emotional management practices, anytime emotion is triggered within you. You will need to be willing to intentionally work with your emotions every day so that you can acknowledge, process, and release your emotions on a day-to-day basis. In doing so, you are allowing yourself to release your emotional reserves to not hold onto them longer than necessary. You also allow yourself to create space for you to learn from your emotions and discover new ways to deal with them more healthily and productively. As you will discover over time, your emotions are something that you will continually learn from every single day. The process of learning how to navigate emotions healthily and productively lasts a lifetime, largely because every time an emotion is triggered, it will be under different circumstances. The more emotion is triggered, especially under different circumstances, the more you become aware of how those emotions feel for you, and how you can navigate those emotions more effectively.

There are many ways that you can create a daily emotional management ritual for yourself, with no one answer being right or wrong. The key to finding a ritual that works best for you is to identify what your life tends to look like from an emotional point of view and to create a ritual that works best for you. An ideal ritual should address how you feel and help you learn from and release those emotions all at once. If you are dealing with a particularly troubling emotion, your daily ritual should include some form of activity intended for helping you process that emotion, too. This way, you are always working within your needs and supporting your overall and day-to-day emotional wellbeing.

Stay Committed to Your Daily Mindfulness Ritual

The first thing you can do for yourself, from an emotional capacity, is staying committed to your daily mindfulness ritual. Mindfulness is going to help you in countless ways, including processing and releasing emotions. A great way to incorporate mindfulness specifically into your daily emotional management ritual is to use mindfulness to help you recognize what emotions you are experiencing and to navigate them in an intentional capacity. The more mindful you are, the more you will find meaningful ways to address your emotions during your emotional release. One great way to incorporate mindfulness into your emotional management routine is to take the time to mindfully investigate any emotions you have experienced throughout your day. You can start by noticing one to three emotions you may have experienced that day that was particularly strong for you. Do not work through any more than three at a time, though, as you do not want to overwhelm yourself and make it more challenging for you to address your emotions. Once you have noticed these emotions, give yourself time to analyze why they occurred, what happened once they did, and how the aftermath of those emotions was experienced. If you can identify the trigger of the emotions, understand your thoughts and feelings in response to those emotions, and recognize how they lead to your behavior. This will give you a greater understanding of how those emotions affected you. Likewise, if you can acknowledge your emotions' consequences, you can create the opportunity for you to understand how your emotional responses affected you in the long run. Be sure to do this for both negative and positive emotions, as this will give you a chance to identify opportunities for growth while also giving you a chance to celebrate yourself for the growth you have already implemented.

Take Up Journaling

Journaling is a wonderful practice for many different reasons. Aside from helping you keep a little log of your life, journaling allows you to express your true thoughts and emotions outside of yourself, where you otherwise may not have been able to. Many people talk about what they truly think and feel seems impossible, even if they are talking to someone such as a therapist where it seems like you "should" be able to speak honestly about what you are thinking or feeling. Having a private journal that you keep to yourself can be a great way for you to openly admit to how you were truly feeling, what you were truly thinking, and anything else that you may have hidden during your day. You can also honestly reflect on what you think and feel after the fact. Releasing your thoughts from your mind and physically getting them out onto paper may not be quite the same as talking to someone about your emotions, but it will provide you with a great opportunity to get a sense of release. In many cases, the sooner you can release your feelings by admitting them, and the more honestly you can do so, the easier it will be for you to let go and move on in the long run. However, if you get into the habit of acknowledging your emotions and then repressing them, it will become more challenging for you to release how you feel about that particular situation. Hence, the pent-up experience begins.

If you are not someone who typically journals, rest assured that there does not need to be a right way or a wrong way for you to engage in journaling. You do not have to be thoughtful, emotional, curious, or well-articulated to keep a journal. You also do not need to worry about spelling, grammar, punctuation, or other writing errors. You don't even need to worry about writing full-form sentences, sharing things in story form, or otherwise being exhaustive in what you are thinking and feeling. Even just keeping bullet-point styled notes about what you were thinking and feeling and how that impacted you can be plenty to help you sort through what is going on in your brain. Use your journal in a way that works for you, and trust that this will be plenty to help you fully accept, learn from, and release any emotions you have experienced on a day-to-day basis.

Work in Harmony with Your Nature

Whenever you try to do something, it is always best to work with your nature rather than against it. In particular, with emotions, working with your nature means rather than denying your emotions or trying to force them to change, you learn to incorporate them into your daily experience. Incorporating your emotions into your daily routines could include fitting certain parts of your routines into certain parts of your day and scheduling your days based on how your feelings behave.

When it comes to scheduling with your energy, consider how you tend to have energy during the day and schedule your activities based on that. This way, you are not trying to force yourself to engage in things when you do not have adequate energy for them. Therefore you have no reason to feel pressured or stressed in those activities. For example, if you know that you tend to have more energy in the morning and less in the evening, you could exercise in the morning and do your mindfulness routine in the evening. If, however, you are the opposite and you tend to have less energy in the morning and more in the evening, you might benefit from doing your mindfulness practice in the morning and exercising in the evening. This way, you are working with your nature to create harmony and flow throughout your day, and you are not amplifying your stress for any reason.

You can also schedule your days based on how you anticipate you will feel. For example, let's say you are trying to schedule your week out, and you know that you have a stressful project to complete on Tuesday. Based on this knowledge, you might make Monday and Tuesday relatively relaxing days and save other things, such as cleaning the house or engaging in other demanding activities later, once the project has already been finished. This way, rather than forcing yourself to get anything done when you already know that you won't have the energy, you work with your nature instead.

As far as emotional fulfillment efforts go, focus on learning tools that allow you to release emotions in a way that can easily be executed on a day-to-day basis. Exercise, art, listening to music, relaxing, talking to a loved one, and other similar measures can all be used to release your emotions in a healthy, productive manner. Suppose you tend to experience many rapid emotions during the day. In that case, you might even consider carrying a journal with you and quickly jotting things down anytime you come across a large feeling. This way, you can quickly release that feeling at the moment, and you can reasonably circle back to it later on in the day. This would be far healthier than, say, stuffing it down and allowing it to ruin the rest of your day.

Master Your Emotions to Defeat Negativity

What steps can you take to master or take charge of your emotions? Let us find out:

Relax and Take Deep Breaths

The minute you perceive something like "dangerous," "upsetting," "frustrating," or "stressful," your entire body tightens up and catapults you into the "fight, flight or freeze" mode. This mode is triggered every time you encounter a challenge, obstacle, or problem. Various physiological reactions occur, such as the tightening of muscles and rapid flow of blood to your muscles to help you cope with the challenge. The coping mechanism mostly involves fleeing the problem or fighting it, and sometimes you even freeze in the situation, but that is the extreme, worst-case scenario.

Stop Reacting to the Emotion

Negative thoughts strengthen in intensity every time you react to them. If you feel angry with your kid and react to the anger by yelling at them, or if you throw a huge fit in reaction to something demeaning your sibling said to you, you will only feel more upset, remorseful, and frustrated later. Reacting to something means you pay heed to the very first irrational thought you experience. To illustrate, if you feel a strong urge to quit your job when your boss does not give you the raise he promised, you may quit your job without thinking about the implications of this decision.

Give Your Emotions Some Time and They Will Calm Down

Try to understand the message it is trying to convey to you. If you are angry with yourself for not qualifying for the next round of an entrepreneurial summit and have lost the chance of winning the grand prize of $1 million, observe your anger and assess it. Ask yourself questions such as: Why do I feel angry? What does the loss mean to me? Asking yourself such questions helps you calm down the strong emotion and let go of the negative thoughts you experienced during that time. Naturally, when you stop focusing on the intense emotion and the negative thoughts it triggers and diverts your attention towards questions to find a way out of the problem, you gently soothe your negative thought process.

Challenge the Negative Thoughts and Replace Them With Positive Ones

It is only when you become aware of your negative thoughts, challenge them, and constantly replace them with positive substitutes that you train yourself to control your extreme emotions and move past them. Here is how you can do this:

Every time you find yourself catastrophizing the severity of an instance, reading too much into things, reducing someone who hurt you to a two-dimensional label, and making pessimistic predictions about things, you do not feel too excited about, question the authenticity of those thoughts and emotions. For instance, if you see your friend losing interest in your conversation, and you jump straight to the conclusion that they hate you or no longer wish to be your friend, hold on to that thought and question its genuineness.

Importance of Habits in Controlling Your Emotions

Assessing your emotional state is a crucial step in honing emotional intelligence and having empathy in general. Some people may be constantly cued into their emotional states, while some others may go a day or a week without thinking about it at all. Although it may be easy to fall into the trap of generalizations about the sort of people who think about their emotions and those that do not, the issue is not as straightforward as it may seem.

People who report that they think about their emotions frequently may be characterized as the sensitive, empathic sort. These are the type of people who naturally ask others how they are feeling or who encourage others when they hear the news that suggests that the other may be going through a trying time. Some people naturally recognize their emotional state, which can lead them to be sensitive to the emotional states of others.

Yet, the distinction between those that recognize their own emotions and those that are thought not to is not as clear cut as the person who gets their parking spot stolen and cries about it, and the other individual who does the "dastardly deed" and laughs with a sense of callous triumph. Sure, there are people like that in the world, and many of us have interacted with them. Movies tend to exaggerate characters because they only have a limited amount of time to show you who someone is, and they have to drive the point home.

But the reality is that even people who do not recognize their emotions or lack empathy may not be as heartless as we believe they are. This discussion is being explored for some reasons, but mostly to introduce you to the idea that the various components of emotional intelligence and empathy are related. Recognizing your emotions is essential as an individual skill. Still, it should be used in tandem with having empathy, identifying the feelings of others, self-regulation, and all the other skills that fall under the scope of emotional intelligence.

We mean that recognizing your emotions has the greatest value if you then use that as a starting point to identify the emotions of others. Recognizing your feelings is also an essential component of self-regulation, which, as you recall, refers to the ability to halt or redirect your own dysfunctional emotions. If you recognize your feelings but then proceed to ignore the feelings of others, acting only with concern to how you think and how you feel, then you may simply be being narcissistic, which is a world away from exercising empathy.

The character that is behaving insensitively may be recognizing her feelings. Recognizing your feelings does not necessarily mean that you care deeply about the feelings of others. As we stated above, the significance of identifying your feelings in the context of emotional intelligence and empathy is that you, in turn, use that to understand the feelings of others, show compassion, and have empathy. The character who is insensitive to the feelings of others may have felt emotions that guided her actions in contrast to what the viewer assumes.

The problem here is that recognizing your own emotions does not necessarily mean that you behave in a way that indicates sympathy for the emotions of others. Narcissist is sensitive to their own emotions and desires, but that does not make them kind, caring, and compassionate people. A narcissist cares only about their passions and motivations and acts with wanton disregard for the emotions and desires of others. A person who recognizes their feelings but does not then assess, understand, and care about the feelings of others is exercising narcissistic behavior, which is harmful and insensitive to the individuals that find themselves in the narcissist's path.

This is an important distinction because some people focus on recognizing emotions and acting on them as a critical emotional intelligence and empowerment tool. Still, all this endeavor does is justify and encourage narcissism. Someone who decides that their sibling or child who has recently been in a car accident cannot come to stay with them temporarily because it is inconvenient may be recognizing their own emotions and acting on them. Still, they may be straying into the narcissistic territory.

It is important to explore this narcissistic dimension of recognizing emotions because this is a behavior pattern that is not only not empathy but in direct opposition to empathy. By behaving narcissistically, we suck all of the empathy out of ourselves and others. We create a world where individuals are motivated by rage, personal gain, spite, and revenge. The power of empathy and emotional intelligence lies in using emotions to form connections with people. If you care only about your feelings and are insensitive to others, you are not creating relationships, you are destroying them.

Self-Regulation Should Work in Concert With Recognizing Your Emotions

Regulating your own emotions will involve understanding what the results of acting on your feelings are. You can also think of this as the implication of your feelings. Your emotions may lead you to engage in an act that is beneficial to you but harmful to someone else. Your feelings may also show you to act impulsively, and acting impulsively frequently leads to actions that we later live to regret. By recognizing your own emotions in concert with self-regulation, you ensure that you behave in a way that considers how others are affected by your actions. Behaving in this self-regulating manner prevents us from conducting narcissistically. By taking a moment to stop ourselves from acting based on emotion, we can then take the important step of assessing the results of our actions. Although it may seem time-consuming to do one mental task after another constantly, this will eventually become second nature. People who have empathy naturally or long practiced have empathy immediately think about the implications of their actions on others. The real power of recognizing your own emotions is assessing what those emotions mean in the bigger picture of human interaction.

Recognizing and Managing Your Emotions

Before you can learn to manage emotions, you need to understand them. You need to know why some emotions are strong while others are weak. At the same time, emotions are an integral part of every person's wellbeing. Whether you are experiencing a good laugh over something or feeling frustrated when you are stuck in traffic, you need to know that the highs and lows that you experience will affect your wellbeing ultimately.

You need to be able to regulate your emotions and even change the way you feel so that you don't affect the people around you negatively. For instance, if you react negatively to something that someone has said crudely, you will attract unwanted attention and even risk your life while at it.

So, how do you get to manage your emotions in the right way? Let us look at a few pointers to this fact:

Tune into Your Feelings

Many people fail to notice the moment until it is gone. Many times, we find ourselves disconnecting from our emotions in such a way that we don't make things work for us. For you to effectively manage your emotions, you need to notice when the emotions happen. Make sure you can pay attention to your feelings the right way before you can move ahead.

Rewind

When you tune into your emotions, you need to take a few steps backward. Ask yourself how you got to the situation that might have contributed to those feelings, and then go after them.

Once you understand where the emotions are coming from, you will manage them the right way. When you notice your emotions, you will be able to look for the various triggers that may have taken you into the feelings in the first place.

Gain the Right Perspective

Once you understand your feelings, the next thing is to step out of the zone and then gain a better perspective. Consider what might happen if you continue in the same vein. What will happen if you stay on the same route that you are following?

Become Self Aware

You cannot manage your emotions when you aren't aware of yourself. You need to tune in and then gain a broader perspective of your emotions. You need to take things deeper and zoom into the moment. Although everyone experiences emotions, the unique experience is subjective in all ways. When you become self-aware, you will understand yourself and come up with the best coping skills.

Listen to the Voices in Your Head

What do you hear? Do you hear anything in your head or your mind? If you can listen to whatever it is, then be able to enumerate it. Give it a name and a volume. Listening to the different voices within your inner self will help you assess the connections between thoughts and feelings. In social situations, especially conflicts, we often make our narrative louder than others.

Change What You Can

You need to cut down on the triggers of the emotion, and you will find that you experience emotions less frequently. This can include cutting down on stress at work, changing negative thought patterns that you experience, and practicing better communication.

Finding an Outlet

When you make changes in your life, you can cut down on any negative emotions that you experience. When you find an outlet, you also eliminate any stress triggers that you might have. When you make changes in your life to reduce frustration, you will find healthy outlets that will deal with the emotions.

There are various outlets that you can use to release negativity. These include:

- Regular exercise gives you an emotional lift as well as the proper outlet for your negativity.
- Meditation will help you to find the much-needed inner peace that you can work with. This activity will make your emotions less overwhelming.

Find various opportunities to have a lot of fun and get more laughter into your life so that you relieve stress and change the perspective of your emotions.

You don't have to stick to these outlets; you can create your own to find something that works best for you.

Experience the emotions, but don't get stuck in them. Managing emotions doesn't mean that you suppress them. What you need to do in such a case is to try and experience the emotion and then let it go. Don't put your mind or your feelings into it because then it will destroy you.

Changing Your Emotions

In some way, emotions always affect a person's thoughts, actions, and moods. They help you to make decisions about what happens in your world. They make you move towards those events, people, and things that excite you and away from the things that make you feel bad.

Every person is capable of experiencing a wide array of feelings, attitudes, and emotions. There are primary emotions and secondary emotions. People always appreciate positive emotions like joy, happiness, affection, and love. However, they always seek to change the negative ones like anxiety, sadness, depression, and the like. The more intense a negative emotion becomes, the more willing a person is to change it. Several ways have been used previously to change moods and emotions that you can apply to your day-to-day life.

One of these techniques is the use of cognitive restructuring. This technique helps individuals to change their thoughts as a way of improving their emotions and mood. It involves the act of suppressing negative thoughts. The procedure works through changing the underlying cause of negative emotion.

When applied to situations regularly, it minimizes the frequency of occurrence for negative moods and prevents those already existing from becoming worse.

Where this technique is not applicable, you can involve other methods to ensure positive results. Most of the encounters that people go through are often stored in the brain, and once you reflect on an encounter, the mind accesses it and replays the actions the same way they occurred. If you keep remembering a negative occurrence, you may end up replaying certain negative feelings since these have also been registered in your brain.

One great attribute of the brain is that it can only recall those occurrences that a person wants to remember. For instance, if you are agitated, the memory may replay every incident or event that agitated you previously, and this may increase the intensity of your anger. The more you think about these occurrences, the angrier you will become.

Other ways that you can employ when seeking to change your emotions include:

- **Take action:** For instance, moving away from the person, event, or environment causing negative emotion.
- **Create a starting point:** Switch to something that makes you think positively. For instance, if you are sad, you can listen to uplifting music.

Emotions form an essential part of human beings, and everyone must understand how to handle them. Most individuals do not like them, especially the negative emotions that may cause anger, pain, sadness, and the like. Because everyone tries to avoid unpleasant feelings, it is common for people to suppress negative feelings, yet this is not advisable. They see such emotions as problems that need to be resolved. However, emotions occur naturally, and it is impossible to suppress them.

The ultimate solution to managing unpleasant feelings lies in learning how to manage one's emotions. Doing this enables you to handle and manage your moods and feelings with success. The process involves accepting a person's emotional state and working on each emotion as it arises.

Since emotions occur in the present, it is also essential that you handle them by dealing with the cause of such emotions. Occasionally, you will experience feelings that are on a dangerous extreme. These can either be negative or positive. With some right strategies, you can adjust such emotions to a moderate level, thus negating any adverse effects.

Negative emotions, in particular, may quickly get out of control as soon as they are triggered. They may also grow to a level that clouds your decision and thinking patterns. They may also occur too frequently when not managed. So, you need to avoid them by mastering even those ill emotions that arise from some harsh circumstances.

Every person experience emotion in one way or another. Some of the emotions are easy to deal with, while some require some extra effort to manage. For every emotion, you must be equipped with the right skills to be able to handle it.

Label Each Emotion

If you would like to manage your emotions effectively, you must first start by acknowledging their existence and any effects they are causing on you. For instance, you need to establish whether you feel disappointed, nervous, excited, or afraid. Note that some emotions may occur as a result of another hidden passion. For instance, a feeling of anger may be due to an action that left you vulnerable or wasted. Dig deep to understand what is exactly happening inside you. Give a label to every emotion that you experience. This is because some people experience multiple emotions simultaneously.

Adjust Your Way of Thinking

Most emotions always affect a person's thought pattern. For instance, if you are anxious about something and the person causing the anxiety calls, you may think something negative will occur. If you are enthusiastic about someone and the person contacts you, you will only develop positive thoughts about what the person will say to you.

Once you have identified and labeled your emotions, filter your thoughts to ensure that you develop a more positive view of the present circumstances. For example, if you feel anxious and your boss calls you at work, avoid thinking about negative things like getting some warning letter or being fired. Instead, keep assuring yourself that there is something positive that will come out of the interaction. Ask yourself what another person would do if they were faced with the same challenge. This will help control your thoughts by changing the function of your brain.

Engage in Suitable Activities

Each time you are faced with a challenge that is causing you to have a foul mood, do not continue to engage in things that make the situation worse. Instead, get some activities that can help uplift your spirit and participate in them.

Avoid Instant Reaction

When it comes to negative emotions, you shouldn't react immediately. This is because when you are angry or in fear, you will always do or say regrettable things. To achieve this, always take a deep breath and relax when faced with a tough situation.

Seek Guidance

Most people find the solution to their feelings by expressing themselves to others. By doing this, you can release your negative emotions to others healthily and acceptably. Recount the occurrences that triggered the emotion and hear what others have to say. This will launch a new perspective on the whole issue, and you can use this insight to manage your thoughts and reactions.

Broaden Your Perspective

Every situation always has a bigger picture that you can focus on. Understand that everything happens for a reason. This will help you see the purpose of any situation instead of focusing on the negative aspects involved. For some circumstances, you may not understand the meaning at the time of occurrence, but as days go by, you may start seeing the reason why things happened as they did.

Practice Forgiveness

Forgiveness also helps you control any actions that would have resulted from the emotion. For instance, if someone wrongs you and you do not forgive the person, you may stay angry for days, weeks, and even years. Constantly getting reminded of other people's misdeeds is what results in repeated wrong actions.

Always Anticipate a Negative Emotion

It will be a lie for you to believe that life will always be pleasant all through. And that you can live a life that is free of pain. Some people seem to be happy all the time.

However, this does not mean that they do not experience any negative feelings. It only means that such people have learned to manage their emotions more effectively. Therefore, always expect some negative feelings to arise as you go about with your day-to-day activities.

Be Flexible

When it comes to emotions, it is almost impossible to control how and when they occur. You need to remain open to these as they occur. Allow them to occur at anytime and anywhere. Only seek ways to balance them so that you do not mess in your actions.

View any negative feelings as an opportunity to improve on yourself. These may be feelings such as fear, anger, jealousy, and anger. Focus on the positive aspect of such feelings; take them as your areas that need development.

Do Not Neglect Any Feelings

Learn how to tolerate any unpleasant sensations. Do not avoid or ignore them. Instead, keep reflecting on the experience and any changes occurring in your body because of such feelings. Keep reminding yourself that millions of people around the globe face the same kind of feelings.

As you do this, ensure that you do not play any blame games towards others. Blaming other people for your negative emotions can hinder them from genuinely interacting with you. Since the feeling has already occurred, it makes no sense to label right or wrong. This is always common when a close associate has triggered the feeling. Most people do this as a way of making themselves feel better, but this strategy never works. Instead, it kills relationships.

Generally, managing emotions is not an easy affair. Sometimes, some feelings may get out of control however much you try. However, the more you practice how to regulate your emotions, the more stable you become when it comes to handling them. With time, you will build your confidence around people and adverse circumstances since it will be easy for you to overcome most of the challenges that you encounter.

CHAPTER 8:

Self-Esteem

There are several strategies that you can implement to enhance your self-confidence and boost your self-esteem. Here are some of them:

- ***Re-affirm your positive traits:*** Just as we often think negative things about ourselves, we must learn to affirm positive traits as well. For example, maybe you're constantly telling yourself, "You're a lazy person." You've been telling yourself that for so long that you are believing it and you've internalized that voice. To see yourself positively and improve your self-esteem, try telling yourself the opposite.
- ***Avoid comparisons:*** One of the toughest parts of developing your self-esteem is realizing that you cannot compare yourself to others. Too often, we compare ourselves with people around us like family, co-workers, friends, or people we don't even know thanks to the exposure to social media. Whether it's about looks, money, personal possessions, or whatever it may

be, the trap of comparing is that you never feel good enough.

- ***Identify your unique gifts:*** Everyone has something that they excel at. We all have our strengths and our weaknesses. Instead of focusing on your weaknesses, focus on what your strengths are and what skills you possess that make you feel confident. Whether it's your skills at work, your creative outlets, your skill on the guitar, or how well you cook, it's important that you are not ashamed of what you do well and channel that energy, so you feel confident about yourself. Don't focus on your failures, focus on your successes! Be proud of your accomplishments.

- ***Focus on self-care:*** Whether you are exercising, treating yourself to a spa day, or getting a good night's sleep, you must take care of yourself physically to take care of your mental health. Exercise is proven to release serotonin, a neurotransmitter of the brain that creates feelings of happiness and contentment. Whether it's an hour at the gym or just going for an evening walk before dinner, take some time to exercise so you are physically taking care of yourself. Do something relax for yourself after a long week. Treat yourself to a cheat day if you've been sticking to your diet regularly. Whatever it is, you should focus on yourself and making your emotional and mental health a priority.

- ***Help others:*** Studies show that helping someone else or volunteering can help you feel better about yourself. It takes you out of your mindset and urges you to think about someone else. The best way to increase your feelings of self-worth is volunteering face to face, such as at a homeless shelter or a soup kitchen. But if you can also donate money or provide services online, then you can also increase your self-worth. You can feel like you are part of a cause and that you are helping people. You have a purpose. This gives value to you and your time, and you feel part of a greater community. This increases your self-worth and self-esteem and how you feel about yourself.

- ***Remind yourself that you are not your circumstances:*** Tell yourself over and over that even if you are going through a tough time right now, you may not be soon. Circumstances occur in our life that is sometimes out of our control. As the saying goes, "this, too, shall pass." With hard work, compassion, and patience, whatever tough time you are going through will soon ease itself. Your problems will be solved, and you will feel stronger for having gone through them. This is important to recognize your self-esteem and not let the circumstances around you beat you down.

CHAPTER 9:

How To Solve Conflict in Your Relationship

Conflicts and arguments are normal aspects of relationships. Sometimes, these fights help the couple come closer and understand each other's needs on a deeper level. However, the same conflicts and arguments can become the reason for separation and even divorce. But before we do all that, let's learn why people fight and what things they fight about when they are in a relationship.

Why Are We Fighting All the Time?

Just a few hours ago, we were this happy couple who no one would think could stay apart for 1 minute, and now we don't want to see each other's faces even. Perhaps it was something that your partner said or did that pushed the buttons. Or maybe they triggered something within you, like a bad memory or thought that just angered you.

Fighting with a partner seems so easy. Sometimes, as natural as talking or laughing together over something silly. After all, they are the closest ones to us. Naturally, we always walk up to them to share our deepest secrets and feelings. They are the closest we have to a family.

Let's get one thing straight first. EVERY COUPLE FIGHTS—even those who say they don't. You are not alone if you think that you are dealing with the toughest and most arrogant partner who hurt you by saying the meanest things to you during a fight. Every partner feels they are living with one or, worse, are that partner themselves. Fighting is a sign of being a typical couple, and to just take away the feelings of guilt and regret away from you, let's put all the blame on your brain, shall we?

Now that we understand how our mind perceives fighting, it is only fair that we acknowledge the reasons most couples fight so that an argument can be prevented before it even begins.

Below are 7 of the most common reasons for fights between married and unmarried couples. Let's discuss these in detail and see how you can gracefully counter them instead of jumping right into it with the same passion as your partner's.

1. Money

Fighting over money is very common among couples. Some fights are about how a partner spends too much on something or how one should save up. Invest it, lock it up in a bank, or buy ourselves a vacation. The options are endless, but opinions may collide. Sometimes partners also have the habit of judging one another over the choices they make. Did you buy $50 worth of imported coffee beans? You should have tipped the waiter more. We must get new flooring as soon as our paychecks roll in. No, we need to get the leaky pipes fixed first.

And then, there are also fights over whether one should have a joint account or not and how to create a monthly or weekly budget.

Solution: Take a deep breath, sit down, and talk about it. Take out a few hours from the weekend and discuss at great length what needs to be done and how. To set a weekly budget, write down all these expenses made in the week, both big and small. Once you have everything sorted out, make it a practice to live by it. Going overboard a little is acceptable but try to remain without the boundaries. At the same time, have an emergency budget as well, just in case. Every time you save some cash from the weekly budget, you can add to the emergency budget or treat yourself with a dinner date.

2. Kids

Children are another common topic over which couples can start fighting. It can be about how they should be raised, their expenses, spending quality time with them, or helping them out with their homework, *etc.* Some partners want to raise their children in a specific way. Often parents from different religions or backgrounds fight over how they should be raised, which religion they should follow, which values and traditions they should hold dear, and so on.

Again, you first need to sit down and ponder over this deeply. The kids are the ones who will be most affected by the fights you have over them. You love them and therefore want the best for them. But at the end of the day, you need to understand that no matter how much you want to control their lives, they will eventually choose their path. That being said, you should mutually lay some ground rules for them to abide by so that they grow up to be sensible and responsible adults.

3. Time

All of these are complaints one partner may have with the other, which can easily start a fight. In almost all relationships, one person wants to spend time with their partner, and when they feel that their partner lacks a similar interest in them, it can lead to frustration. Thoughts like "someone doesn't like me anymore" can stir in one's mind, increasing discomfort.

Some fights can also be about how partners choose to spend their time together. One partner might want to go to a movie, whereas the other partner might want to go to the game. One might want to go hiking, whereas others might want to spend the weekend with their family.

Instead of fighting over how you two want to spend 24 hours of the day, join forces and dedicate a "together time" for every day or the weekend. The goal shouldn't be to prioritize one's interests over the others but rather to find a middle ground. Do things you both enjoy doing, such as partying or going out for dinners.

4. Priorities

"You never give me time. You are always busy on the phone. You are always going out with your friends, but you never take the kids or me out." The expressions mentioned before are messages that can alert you that your relationship is not passing by a good moment. There are times when partners may start to think that they are no longer a priority in the lives of their spouses. There are no flowers anymore, no unexpected hugs or kisses, or demand for intimacy in the middle of the night. Your partner may be working extra hard just so that they can provide for the family better. Their priority may no longer be just you. So instead of fighting over it, talk it out. Let them know that you miss the old times and how you two should try to spend some time at least together. Also, make it a rule to limit the use of phones when home so that the two of you can connect.

5. Sex

The lack of sex or less of it can easily trigger an argument or fight amongst couples. Since everyone has a different need and libido for sexual intimacy, you might feel left out if your partner rarely initiates it. Perhaps, they are too tired and just want to get to bed. Perhaps, there is so much going on in their heads that sex doesn't find a spot. Perhaps, they think that you no longer enjoy it, or sex has become tedious for you. There are a dozen reasons why sex can lead to fights, arguments, and even separation.

Thus, understand each other's needs for intimacy and try to meet halfway. Also, instead of being quiet about your needs and wants, openly express your concerns regarding the lack of intimacy and how it is affecting your mental state.

6. The Past

"You haven't forgotten about her, have you? You still are in love with your ex. Why do you keep comparing me with your ex in everything?"

Often, this thought can be very damaging when it is you that keeps comparing yourself with your significant other's ex. The more you nag about it, the more it will frustrate your partner. If the past, in any way, hurt your partner, it is best not to bring it up in a fight, and you will only be hurting them on a deeper level. You two must, at all times, maintain a certain respect for each other's privacy, emotions, and past and not let it get between you two and cause a rift.

7. Chores

"You still haven't fixed the dishwasher; how many times do I have to remind you? Why is there an empty carton of milk in the refrigerator? You could have at least taken out the trash. Why is everything my job?"

Your partner may have a different concept of cleanliness than you. You need to accept that. Hair in the bathtub or the sink may not drive them crazy, or they choose to let go of it. On the other hand, you might find it annoying if they drink right from the carton or forget to place the newspapers where the other stack is every day.

If you sense that your partner isn't too enthusiastic about certain chores like taking out the trash or putting the kids to bed, ask them to help you in some other way. Divide the chores accordingly so that peace can be restored in the house.

Wait...Are You Saying That Fighting Is Healthy?

Some couples don't fight because they fear it would cause them to hate each other. They think that the risks of speaking up would only lead to disrupting the peace of the house and their relationship, so they remain quiet and accept things as fate. However, we fail to consider the danger of not speaking up and how it would ultimately mess up the relationship. A lack of communication is a primary reason for failed relationships. Speaking your mind, even if it comes in the form of an argument, is beneficial to help you two overcome the differences of ideas, opinions, and thoughts. Not addressing the elephant in the room and pretending that everything is fine will impact your intimacy and trust in your partner. So, discussing the underlying issues is the way to a happier and more fulfilling life with a partner. When sensitive issues are discussed rather than fought about later, it gives both partners peace of mind and helps them grow together. The act of fighting can also make one realize the importance of the partner's feelings and avoid hurting them again by repeating the mistake made.

The 4 Good Fights!

Not every argument means that it's time to head for the door. Arguments can be settled with some pondering and analyzing what led to it in the first place. As soon as you identify the mistake, you will try your best to avoid it. Because let's face it, fighting hurts. Although no couple would deliberately like to go at it, sometimes, fighting can be good for your relationship.

Take a look at these 4 types of fighting that help rekindle the fizzled love and respect you craved from your partner.

Fights That Spark Awesome Makeup Sex

We have seen it in some of our favorite room coms and wished it would happen with us. Remember **Mr. and Mrs. Smith**, anyone? Did that makeup sex scene after that home-shattering fight not have you wishing you had something this passionate with your partner once? The reason makeup sex is so awesome and passionate is that the partners still possess the same energy and fire they emitted from within themselves during the argument. So, you can expect the same passion under the sheets.

So, remember, not every fight has to have a bad ending; some just tend to have a sexier finish as well.

Fights That Resets Boundaries

Sometimes, we end up crossing a line that we shouldn't have during an argument. It can be something you said that hurt your partner deeper, and you instantly regretted saying it. It can be a harsh reminder of their failure, their poor sexual performance, or just a direct hit to their character that catches them off guard and ends up hurting them.

That very instant when this realization hits you is the moment you understand how it must be like to be in your partner's shoes right now. Had you two not been arguing, you would have never known the extent of how much your words can hurt your partner and also help you realize a mistake that you don't want to be repeating anytime soon!

Fights Where You Promise to Treat One Another Better

You have ever argued so intensely that you both regret it? Was it hard to move past that and look at each other in the eye again? Many couples, after a fight, realize how damaging it was for their relationship and swear to treat each other better the next time around—the kind of a dispute that almost turned physical or meant the end of your relationship. Someones just go to a point where the couple finally concludes that something major needs to be done here to fix it.

These kinds of disagreements are the best because they make you realize that you didn't consider the feelings of your spouse and thus vow to treat them better.

Fights Where You Two Learn Something About Each Other

If you listen carefully, an argument with a partner can be a great source of new information for you. Thus, use your mind when listening to what they say. Perhaps they felt hurt over a random joke you made. Since you wouldn't want them to feel insulted or humiliated, your goal will be to avoid repeating it. But how did you learn about it? During a fight, right? So, in a way, arguments can help the two of you to understand each other better.

CHAPTER 10:

Actions Needed to Overcome the Conflict Between Couples

When faced with a conflict in your growing relationship, think about how you express your feelings or talk about this conflict with your partner. Good communication is where everyone can take stock and try to understand the attitude of the other. The conflict will be easier to manage when angry tones and unnecessary insults do not exacerbate it.

For effective conflict communication, there are three rules to follow:

- Avoid raising your voice and keep calm whenever a conflict happens.
- Allow your partner to talk and develop their argument because communication involves talking and listening.
- Find a middle ground, but do not make compromises that can negatively affect the future.

A couple who argues but who respects these three rules will find it easier to resolve a resolution.

Relationships are not always easy, and you are continually learning. Is it possible not to repeat the same mistakes and stabilize one's romantic relationship? How can you manage conflicts in your relationships without becoming a doormat?

Follow these recommendations to rebuild the love in a struggling relationship:

- Once you understand the reasons for the tensions that are shaking your relationship, you can move on to the more "direct" phase of reconciliation. The first step can, indeed, be very psychological because you have to communicate with your partner.
- It is necessary to place more technical and thoughtful actions to find your partner's heart and overcome your relationship's crisis.
- The actions you have decided to put in place must correspond to the different issues. Otherwise, the latter will not have any particular effects and may perhaps even aggravate the situation. Don't seek resolution just to be done with it, seek resolution to make it better.
- Don't assign blame on either side. Relationships are a team effort, and both of you need to be in it altogether, or not at all.

- If your partner or yourself are not feeling fulfilled in your relationship, you need to spend time together to understand better your issues and what you need from the relationship.

Every relationship experiences conflict at one point or the other. It is essential to know that disagreement is not necessarily a bad thing, it is a way by which people express their diverse views on a situation or topic.

CHAPTER 11:

How to Manage Conflicts

The most complicated and confusing thing to successfully manage in a relationship is conflict. Tensions run high, and at the moment, you both say something you shouldn't to try and "win" the argument. You end up regretting it later, but some things cannot be taken back. It is a challenge for all couples, even those who have been together for decades.

Setting the Right Environment

There must be some level of security and trust in your relationship before you can even begin to talk about the rough stuff with your partner.

If you have hidden important information from them in the past or have been cruel during previous arguments, you have to put in some effort to regain that level ground you two were on in the beginning. The most important ways to create a calm and safe space are pretty simple. You just have to know where to start and what to do.

Trust

The foundation of any relationship is built on mutual trust. Imagine that you plan to go on a cruise. You wonder which company will give you the experience, and the facts are laid out before you. One cruise line has had many issues on several excursions: the power goes out, the sewage tank backs up, and people have gotten food poisoning from the buffet. The other is one you have booked a cruise with before, and you had no major problems on your trip.

Get to the Root of the Issue

This is related to the exploration phase. Don't attempt to sell your viewpoint to your spouse. Talk about underlying problems that contribute to the issue you are trying to resolve. Listen mindfully to your significant half's concerns with an open and flexible mind. Learn everything about yours as well as your partner's issues. Keep your eyes on the bigger picture and form a mental list of concerns.

Pick Your Battles

Sometimes, it is best to drop these smaller issues, given the larger picture. This is when shared meaning, emotional connections, and connection bids can come to the rescue. Even when you don't agree on the smaller things, these more significant shared memories and meaning, along with the number of times you've managed to turn in towards each other's connection bids, prove valuable. As a couple, you are guaranteed not to agree with everything. However, the relationship's overall compatibility, respect, and health (based on the validations and acceptance you've shown each other earlier) depend on how you manage to overcome these differences.

Identify a Middle Ground

Finding a balance or middle ground between what you and your partner seek is critical to a relationship's health.

If both partners are concerned about making the relationship work, you will consciously work towards an agreement. Finding a middle ground is much easier than we think.

Limit Yourself to a Single Hurt

Limiting yourself to a single hurt helps the other person empathize with your feelings more effectively while validating the meaning assigned to the situation, whether demeaning, disrespected, ignored, or not acknowledged. Throwing a bunch of accusations about multiple feelings violated makes the person feel like they are being attacked.

The focus shifts away from the issue to the person. It becomes more of a personal attack than an issue that needs resolution.

Don't Build a Hurt Museum

Don't build a hurt museum over a while. It can destroy the basis of a relationship if the relationship doesn't have enough emotional connections and shared memories to fall back on. Our hurt comprises everything from memories of the past to our partner's hurtful comments to their disappointment. Focus on building shared memories than a hurt museum. Don't keep memories negatively charged in your mind for long.

Don't Hesitate to Enlist External Help

At times, a neutral third-party resolution is all you need to resolve a disagreement or issue. Mediators exist precisely for this objective. Mediators are professionally trained to resolve disputes between couples, and using a professional mediator can lead to a cleaner, faster, and healthier resolution that can be acceptable to both parties.

Stay Away from Negativity

It can be challenging to avoid responding to a partner's bad behavior with worse behavior. Indulging the urge only makes the challenging situation even worse.

Couples that kept a ratio of 5 positive behaviors or attempts at well-meaning humor, warmth, and collaboration to every negative behavior were significantly less likely to separate or divorce after 4 years.

Know When It Is Time for a Timeout

If you view yourself slipping into a negative pattern and find that either you or your partner are not following the above-mentioned strategies, take time out from the argument. Taking a short break with a few deep breaths can be enough to calm tempers. Research on arguments reveals that controlling anger and taking the other person's perspective are important for managing conflicts effectively!

Building Trust Over Time

The best time to begin gaining another person's trust, especially a romantic interest, is right away. No relationship will last long if, after a month, you still haven't done anything to deserve unwavering belief. How do you go about building it, though? It's elementary!

Staying Respectful During Arguments

If you feel guilty thinking back over all the times you have treated your lover badly during heated arguments, try to get to the root of *why* you did it.

Were you feeling insecure about yourself at the time? Insecurity in ourselves and the frustration that comes with it causes us to lash out at our partners. The insults we throw at the people we love are often a mirror of what we are feeling about ourselves. Did the other person say something negative toward you first? The human ego kicks into overdrive when that happens, so we do anything we can to defend ourselves and preserve a sense of pride.

4 Ways to Maintain Respect in a Relationship

There are 4 parts to putting your respect into action and maintaining that peace and harmony in your relationship:

- *Mutuality:* It is the concept of setting up boundaries in your relationship and agreeing to abide by them.
- *Reciprocity: This* ensures that you both promise to keep your judgments and assessments of one another fair and balanced.
- *Accommodate:* This should be done while respecting the other's limitations, even if the formerly agreed-upon boundaries change as you grow and change as individuals.
- *Accept:* You are both different and, therefore, will have different beliefs and dreams.

Remembering and observing these 4 concepts every day will foster a peaceful and happy partnership.

Approaching Difficult Topics

By now, you have successfully created an atmosphere of trust in your home where you both can be vulnerable with each other. From now on, talking things out will be easier. However, every relationship goes through troubles at one point or another, and it's crucial to address the problem and solve it together. Sometimes, the topic is incredibly personal and touchy, and you may have a tough time trying to navigate it. Have no fear!

CHAPTER 12:

How to Restore Balance in a Relationship

Resolving an argument with your significant other? Is that even possible? Won't they just keep bringing it up from time to time? Have you ever met my spouse?

The truth is that settling an argument is fairly easy when both the partners acknowledge the differences in opinions and are ready to address the issues decently. So, let's learn some foolproof means not only to end an argument but settle it once and for all.

Focus on the Present

Arguments are the result of unsettled conflicts from the past. However, trying to bring up something entirely different from what you two are fighting about will only add to the resentment you two have. Avoid doing that and focus on the current issue only. This also goes for all those times when you try to use that past to prove a point or convey a message.

However, if you keep finding yourself bringing past grievances, it means you still aren't over them, and to move forward, you must sit down and resolve them first.

Personalize Your Statements With "I"

Use sentences that emphasize more than a personalized experience rather than a general one. For instance, if you felt insulted when your partner joked about your weight in front of his friends, instead of saying something like, it's disrespectful when you joke about my weight with our guests, say something like, "I felt so disrespected when you joked about my weight in front of your friends. I felt humiliated."

Which of the statements has a deeper impact and yet gracefully delivers the message across? Statements starting with a personalized note, like the word "I," allow your partner to see how hurt you felt.

Avoid Being Passive-Aggressive

Next, try not to act passive-aggressive. This won't help settle any argument-big or small. Passive-aggressive behaviors are poison for communications and only make arguments worse. Instead of expressing your anger with words, you choose behaviors like trying to make one jealous, gossip, pretend they don't exist or cease communicating with them at all. Always choose to speak your mind to resolve the issue as soon as possible without escalating to something bigger. Many partners choose to stay quiet or use a sarcastic tone instead of just saying, "I am mad at you," thus leaving their partners in a mix of confusion and cluelessness as to how to move past this silence.

As stated above, use "I" statements to let your partner know that you have done something to upset them instead of hiding from them or ignoring them. The more open you are, the easier it will become to settle an argument.

Use Suitable Language

Never use derogatory language during an argument, as it will do anything but settle it. The words you choose and how you deliver them are very important in any fight with your partner. You may have a different body language that counters your words. Even when you are in a heated conversation, use appropriate language to express your emotions. You have to stay respectful and ensure that your partner doesn't feel disrespected either. This means that you aren't allowed to name-call them as labels can sting you back in the ass the next time you fight with them.

Even when you think you will lose your mind if you continue with the debate, choose to refrain from using harsh words or cursing. Yelling is also not acceptable at any cost. You have to be extra special with the tone and pitch of your voice because sometimes we don't even realize that we are yelling unless the other person points it out. If you are being told to lower your voice down, do that instantaneously.

Openly Communicate Your Expectations

Be clear about what you expect what your partner needs to do. There is no need to confuse them with riddles or avoid conversing with them just because they did something you didn't like. Sometimes, our words can also have double meanings or be understood in different manners, which is why it is always best to be crystal clear about your expectations when settling an argument with your partner.

Reach Out for Support

If the issue doesn't reach a fruitful conclusion still, maybe you need someone else to intervene and take over. Sometimes, a new perspective can help both partners see the problem from a completely different angle. This is where professional counseling or therapy comes in. Hire a marriage counselor to improve communication. A professional counselor may help you with tips on how to talk to each other without riling up or how to resolves arguments and conflicts.

CHAPTER 13:

Basic for Successful Relationship

Do you find yourself going through a string of failed relationships, while those around you all seem to be happy and content in their marriages?

Do you ever stop to wonder what they are doing differently?

Perhaps, you have now found yourself with a partner you feel you could build a future with and want to do your best to make things last.

We have taken a look at behavioral traits that can damage relationships, but what about the behaviors that strengthen them? What are the secrets of those couples who have made their relationships last for twenty, thirty, forty years, or longer? Is it simply a case of learning to put up with your partner's challenging behaviors?

Or is there much more to it? Couples therapists agree there are several important traits present in successful relationships that all couples should aspire to. Let's take a look:

Forgiving One Another

Many of us have the incorrect belief that forgiving someone means allowing them to get away with whatever they did to us. But this is simply not the case. Forgiving someone does not mean we are not forgoing our need for justice, an apology, or reconciliation. Forgiveness is separate from the three things. Another common misconception is that forgiveness is a sign of weakness, but this is not the case. True forgiveness can be immensely difficult to give and requires a great deal of inner strength. As I'm sure you will agree, this is as far as a weakness as one can get.

Forgiveness can be considered as having two elements: decisional and emotional. Decisional forgiveness occurs when we consciously move from a place of ill will towards a person to wishing them well. We no longer wish for bad things to happen to someone who has hurt us an important first step on the journey. This is most often the easiest element of forgiveness to manage.

But emotional forgiveness goes much deeper. This type of forgiveness takes place when we can actively move away from the negative feelings the wrongdoing invoked in us and replace them with far more positive emotions. This part of forgiveness often takes time, as it is human nature to dwell on negative emotions, and even when we feel we have moved on, they have a tendency to return when we least expect it. This is especially prevalent when our spouse has committed major wrongdoing against us, such as telling lies or being unfaithful. Sometimes even the smallest trigger can lead us to recall events we thought we were over.

Forgiving your partner for their wrongdoings also sends out a powerful message.

When you do so, you are making them aware that you know they did not intentionally set out to hurt you, as there is love between them.

This is an important first step in letting your relationship mend.

Complimenting Your Partner

Regularly complimenting your partner is a simple way to show what you value in your loved one. It contributes to your spouse's positive self-esteem and provides a focus on all that is good about your relationship.

But while complimenting your partner when the two of you alone is great, the relationship can be strengthened by making these positive comments in front of others.

And this needn't be a showy, declaration of all that is wonderful about your spouse. Simple throwaway lines to friends and family such as "My husband made a great dinner last night," or "She always picks up the phone when I call" can go a long way to maintaining closeness and a sense of appreciation within a relationship.

Focusing on the Positives

All relationships have their ups and downs, even the strongest and most loving ones. But for a relationship to be happy and successful, the positive moments must outweigh the negative. Successful couples make a habit of pointing out the positives within their relationship. They thank each other for kind words or actions, give compliments freely, and congratulate one another on their successes.

Similarly, couples tend to be stronger when they laugh a lot. This is a powerful trait that helps prevent life from becoming weighed down with stressors.

Of course, all couples will face serious issues throughout their life, but being able to face challenges with a sense of humor can be a powerful asset.

Understanding Each Other's Differences

Most often, the cracks that form in a relationship are the result of two clashing personality types. We can easily interpret our partner's behavior as an attempt to create conflict or start an argument. But more often than not, disagreements arise because different personalities approach situations in different ways. Something we see as just a normal part of our day-to-day behavior may drive our partner mad; for example, if one habitually messy partner fails to put their clothes away at the end of the day. The tidy partner might misconstrue this as their loved one deliberately being lazy or disrespectful, while for the messy partner, it was merely a subconscious reaction with no deeper motive.

Successful couples invest time in understanding who their partner is, what drives them, what irritates them, and what is important to them. When we develop a deeper understanding of our partner's inherent personality traits, we make it easier to avoid conflict and handle disagreements when they arise more effectively.

Expressing Interest in One Another's Lives

While you and your partner must have independent interests, one of the traits of successful couples is their ability to show interest in their partner's lives. This includes areas such as work-life, friendships, family, and hobbies. Ask questions regularly and listening intently to the answers. This also goes a long way to assure your partner that you are comfortable with the part of their life that you are not involved in.

Flirting With Each Other

Flirting is one of the keys to maintaining an active sex life and a connected and loving relationship outside the bedroom. Even, and especially, for couples who have been together for many years, flirting is a powerful way to show your attraction for your partner and keep the spark alive. When flirting is no longer present, the relationship runs the risk of becoming stale and mundane, both in and out of the bedroom.

Don't Fight Dirty

All couples fight, even the strongest ones. But those in successful relationships ensure that, when things get tense, they do not resort to name-calling, put-downs, or digging up the past. Even when you and your partner disagree, respecting one another is key.

CHAPTER 14:

Why Is Important to Establish Your Relationship Goal

Make it a point to set goals about communication, love, compromise, commitment, sexual intimacy, household chores, and support. These are the main aspects that influence the quality and strength of your relationship. Once you cover these areas and come up with attainable goals, you can improve your relationship.

It is quintessential that you and your partner both work on improving the way you communicate. While setting goals in this area, think about ways in which you can improve your communication.

Take some time, sit down with your partner, and asked them what they need. Emotional support is not the only form of support you can provide your partner with. At times, something as simple as driving your partner to the grocery store or taking them to the dentist are forms of support too. Make sure that you set some time aside to check in with your partner regularly.

For a relationship to last, then there needs to be friendship in it. You must be more than just partners; you must be friends first. Come up with different things you and your partner can do together. Shared activity certainly helps increase your degree of closeness. You and your partner can also take turns selecting different activities you can try out together.

I am certain you love your partner, but how expressive are you? If you don't express your love, how will your partner ever know? How often do you express your thoughts? I'm not suggesting that you need to keep telling your partner repeatedly that you love them, but there are little things you can do which convey your love for them. For instance, sharing in on any household responsibilities, cooking their favorite meal, or hugging them as soon as you wake up in the morning are all ways in which you can show your love for them. In a long-term relationship, it is quintessential that you express your love and affection for your partner.

A relationship will not last if there are no compromises. My way or the highway kind of thinking can quickly shatter any relationship. Instead, learn to compromise. It is okay if you don't always get your way, and it is okay if you are not always right. Start making an effort to understand your partner's perspective. Learn to negotiate and understand the importance of coming to compromises. When you compromise, it doesn't mean that you are wrong while your partner is right, it merely means that you love your partner more and are willing to concentrate on the relationship instead of any other petty issues or problems.

Emotional intimacy is as important as physical intimacy in a relationship. So, make a conscious effort and set certain goals for physical intimacy in your relationship. Be a responsive and caring lover to your partner. Spend some time to discuss with your partner all the various things you want to try and be open with them. Learn to cater to not just your needs, but the needs of your partner as well.

A common problem a lot of couples run into is related to household responsibilities. I believe in the equality of partners, and therefore, partners must share all responsibilities. After all, you are living together, so why not share the responsibilities? Spend some time and come up with a schedule to divide responsibilities between the two of you so that one partner doesn't always feel burdened with household work. This is quintessential, especially if you and your partner have day jobs to attend to as well.

Tips to Keep in Mind

Happiness doesn't always come from getting what you want, but it can come from moving toward what you desire. When it comes to relationships, it essentially means that couples must have a couple of goals they are moving toward together. So, how can couples support and motivate each other to achieve their individual goals along with the relationship goals? Here are some simple steps you can follow to ensure that you and your partner reach your goals while maintaining your relationship's health.

The first step is to ensure that your individual goals are in perfect alignment with your relationship goals. This alignment is quintessential to create a sense of harmony, which allows you both to attain your personal goals. Once this harmony is present, there is no limit to the things you can achieve as a team.

It is time to make two plans: a 6-month plan and a 2-year plan. Think of these as short and long-term goals for your relationship. Discuss what you plan on doing, where you want to be, and how you want to be within these two timeframes. The next step is to visualize and think about where you want your life to be in the next 5, 10, 15, and 20 years. Ensure that you maintain a positive attitude and don't casually write off any ideas until you have both had a chance to express yourself first. Don't judge your partner, and don't allow your partner to judge you. Keep an open mind toward each other and attentively listen to what the other person has to say.

Spend some time and make a list of all your personal goals. You and your partner must do this individually and then spend some time together to discuss the lists you both made.

You can take all the time you need, and carefully note everything you wish to attain in life. Include short-term as well as long-term goals and discuss this if you feel like you're getting stuck while making this list.

Whenever you are setting any goals, the goals must be such that they make you feel good about yourself. If the goal you are setting for yourself or your relationship goes against everything you believe in, you will not be able to achieve it. The goals you set for yourself must not only be good for you but must be good for your relationship as well. When you have shared goals, it not only becomes easier to achieve them, but the health of your relationship also improves along the way.

You and your partner must come up with an arrangement that helps you stay focused and accountable for any commitments you make. The relationship you share with your partner is quite sacred, and you must cherish and nourish it. The arrangements you create must support you and your partner along with your relationship. It's not about getting rewards or punishments to create accountability. It is about coming up with a mutually beneficial plan to create accountability for each other.

It is okay to concentrate on your goals, but it is not okay to overlook any victories you attain along the way. Attaining your goals is seldom a sprint and is always a marathon. So, the journey to your goals matters as much as the goal itself.

You and your partner must be appreciative of each other and each other's accomplishments. Rejoice in all the small wins that happen in your lives. Celebrate each other's successes. By doing this, you are naturally cementing the bond you share. If you celebrate every milestone you cross, it will give you the motivation to keep going.

You must be supportive and understanding. Support and encourage your partner to achieve their goals, and your partner will reciprocate these gestures towards you. Give your partner the room they need to attain their goals and don't become a hurdle. Keep a conscious check on any criticism you dole out. If your partner is making a mistake, feel free to correct them, but do so gently. Be each other's support system. There will be days when you or your partner simply don't have the motivation to keep going. In such instances, be each other's cheerleaders. Your relationship will be happy and more satisfactory when you know you have your partner's support, and the same applies to your partner. Make it a point to seek feedback from your partner to see how they are doing. By asking for their feedback, you are making them feel important and giving yourself a chance to view things from a fresh perspective.

Spend some time and make a note of all your goals. Keep reviewing these goals as you go about your daily life. Your goals can change, or the way you want to achieve them might change. You might also need to tweak your goals occasionally. So, don't forget to include a weekly review session of your goals.

The final step is quite simple: always remember you are a team. Achieving goals becomes easier when you are doing it together. You don't have to do everything by yourself, and you can count on your partner for additional help or support.

Once you have accomplished your dreams or goals, don't forget to come up with new goals. Goals give you the motivation to keep going!

CHAPTER 15:

Exercise to Reduce Anxiety

Positive Thinking

To reduce symptoms of anxiety, there are exercises you and your partner can do. If you are not the one who suffers from anxiety, it is imperative to support your partner. Join him or her in performing these exercises. You might even be surprised how beneficial they can be for the reduction of overall stress.

The exercises are simple, anyone can do them, and they work best if they are combined. Don't choose just one, try them all and see what suits you best. Some should be done every day, others on occasion. But they will have the best result if you find your tempo, get used to the new routine, and enjoy it with your significant other.

Distract Yourself

This exercise is simple, and it doesn't give away the feeling of a task. However, it is difficult to practice it while you are in the middle of an anxiety attack, so keep that in mind.

Sometimes you will lack focus, and other times you won't find these activities as pleasurable.

This is why you should have your partner helping you and joining you whenever it is possible.

Here are some of the activities you could do together:

1. Watch a comedy movie or comedy stand-up show.
2. Exercise together or go for a hike.
3. Clean the house together or work on renovating a room.
4. Try out a new restaurant.
5. Play your favorite game together.

Alternatively, you can come up with your pleasurable activities. The idea is to distract yourself from all of your worries and anxieties with something that gives you pleasure.

The above are just examples, and you do not need to follow them. Make a list. The time will eventually come when it will be challenging to think of an activity you could use to distract yourself from your anxiety.

Make a second list of activities you could do on your own if your partner is not with you at that time. Try crocheting, painting, volunteering, walking a dog, etc.

Mindful Breathing

This exercise will help you practice focusing on the present moment, and it will help you concentrate. Mindful breathing refers to counting your breaths while being aware of each one of them. Breathing is a reflex that nobody thinks about. Breath is life; without it, we wouldn't survive. Bring your breathing to a level of awareness by following a few simple steps:

1. Sit or lie down comfortably in a room that feels safe.
2. Focus on your breathing. Try to discern whether you breathe with your chest or abdomen.
3. Do not try to control your breathing. It has to be natural. Don't control its pace or how much air you take in. This exercise can be challenging as awareness of your breathing often results in an attempt to control it. For now, you need to fight this urge and let it be natural.
4. Keep yourself focused on breathing, your mind may wander, but you have to remind yourself why you are doing this exercise and return your focus to breathing.
5. Finish your mindful breathing in a set time frame. You can set the alarm to remind you the time is up. Stretch your body and notice how you feel. What are your emotions, and are there any intrusive thoughts? Keep in mind that this exercise's point is awareness. It doesn't matter what you are thinking or feeling.

Keep in mind that you will have bad days and good days, so try to practice mindful breathing as often as you can. Start with a 5 minutes' exercise and slowly progress to 10, 20, and 30 minutes. Usually, there is no need for more than that.

Abdominal Breathing

The way an anxious person breathes is fundamental. During an anxiety attack, your breath becomes shallow and comes from your chest. This type of breathing can intensify your symptoms of anxiety.

Shallow chest breathing can also cause hyperventilation, which is similar to a panic attack and will cause even more instability in a person with an anxiety disorder.

Because of this, it is imperative to practice abdominal breathing.

Abdominal breathing will raise oxygen levels in your brain and muscles, and it will stimulate the parasympathetic nervous system, which is responsible for calming you down. The benefits of abdominal breathing can be enormous for people suffering from any anxiety disorder as well as panic attacks.

You could ask your partner to join you in practicing this breathing as it can benefit anyone. Here is how to do it properly:

1. Sit or lie serenely. Spot one hand on your chest and the other on your mid-region. Inhale normally without endeavoring to control it. Notice which hand is rising while you are breathing in.
2. Control your next breath and attempt to make it as profound as conceivable to move the hand that lies on your midsection. Breathe in through your nose gradually.
3. When you are done inhaling, make a pause and count to four once again while holding your breath.
4. Exhale slowly to a count of five. You can exhale through your nose or mouth. It doesn't matter, as long as you feel comfortable.
5. After you completely emptied your lungs, take two normal, natural breaths without controlling them.
6. Repeat each step and continue this cycle for 5 minutes.

Abdominal breathing exercises should be practiced daily. It will calm you down and teach you how to focus. Keep in mind that it is constructive in crises when a panic attack is possible. It will calm you

CHAPTER 16:

Quiz Part: Know Your Level of Attachment and Compatibility

Self-Assessment to Know the Level of Your Attachment

A time comes when you have to commit yourself to a relationship for the long term. A couple needs to look at their relationship and ask themselves some questions:

- How strong is this relationship?
- Which challenges might occur?
- Which problems lie ahead?
- How do we solve them?

Ideally, relationship assessment can be done on a personal level or by the two parties. Some of the things you can look at include:

- Do you argue?
- How are decisions made in your relationship?

- How well do you know your partner?
- Do you assess your future, and are you in agreement about goals and visions?
- Are you compactible?
- Do you agree on the role of the extended family in your relationship?
- Do you get along with the extended family?
- Is your partner your support system and best friend?

Every couple has arguments, misunderstands, and conflicts. The main thing to consider is how well you keep things in control when you argue. Do things get out of hand, or do you manage to circle back and find a viable solution to the problem?

Arguments are unique to every relationship. For some people, arguing involves exchanging4 sentences riddled with emotions, some huffing, and snapping. For others, an argument may include the use of tough cursing words or decibel levels above 16. The most important thing is the ability to put breaks or end a conversation once you feel that it has escalated to an emotionally dangerous battle. If a discussion gets out of hand, one or both of you should be able to walk away or calm things down.

It requires self-regulation and awareness to prevent a conversation from getting out of control. Typically, in the heart of a conflict, we become tunnel-vision and are forced to want to make our point heard by force. This exchange then becomes a battle to the death. When a conversation is going nowhere, it is essential to try to put it back on track. It is okay to get upset, and it is normal for 2 people to disagree, but the most important thing is to catch things before they run out of hand. Are you or your partner able to tame a wild conversation? If you can stop an argument before it burns the relationship down, then you have mastered a critical relationship skill.

On the other hand, some couples do all they can to avoid confrontations. Here is the thing, such couples will avoid confrontation at this minute, but it will blow up in the future. Two people can only walk on eggshells for so long. People cannot live forever without expressing their true feelings because distance is not a solution to disagreements. If you push important emotions to the side, connecting or getting deeply intimate will be tough. In fact, the relationship becomes superficial and disengaged. Those differences that are swept under the carpet will cause one day a spill.

Some couples prefer to end an argument quickly before it turns into a battle. The challenge with this technique is that a lot will be left unsaid, and the solution will not be long-term. For instance, if a person got home late last night and their partner starts a confrontation, the accused partner may prefer to say," I am really sorry about last night," then walk away. That will leave the other person unsatisfied.

It is essential to be able to circle back and finish an argument. Circling back means that if you must end a conversation prematurely for whatever reason, you should be able to go back and solve it when things are better. Step up and solve the conflict effectively.

Decision Making

Decision-making skills are required in every sector of life, especially when you must spend forever with someone who has their own beliefs, values, thoughts, and life. What is your process of sorting out problems? At every stage of a relationship, decisions must be made. Some decisions affect you and those you choose to ignore. For instance, you might not be concerned about interior decoration; therefore, it does not really matter what your partner picks. However, a subject like finance management might affect you; consequently, you want to be involved.

Decision-making is about content, the things we must decide together, and those we can just leave out. It is also about boundaries, who does what, and when. Good decision-making requires the couple to have a constructive and come to an agreement. Besides, you need to understand how everyone processes information to make an informed decision for good decision-making skills. For instance, you might realize that your partner prefers to do a lot of research before making any decisions, which might mean delays.

However, decision-making in a relationship has an underlying issue called power. Who makes the primary decision, and is there equality in the relationship when making decisions? Can every partner give their opinion freely, or is one person in charge of everything? Is there a balance in the relationship, or does one walk on eggshells with anxiety?

Knowing Your Partner

How well do you know your partner? It is imperative to understand the emotions of the person you are in a relationship with. What triggers their anger or joy? What are they sensitive to? Do they handle criticism well? Are they open-minded? Do they speak up when something is bothering them? Knowing your partner involves understanding their past. You might realize that their fear comes from past experiences. Do you know if your partner wants children?

Knowing what your partner likes and what makes them sensitive goes a long way in building the relationship. You will be able to tell if your partner is okay or coming down with something. Furthermore, you will know what to avoid and what to say at a particular time. The thing is, everyone has an emotional pothole, and it is best to avoid them. Everyone has at least one emotional wound they prefer to conceal or protect. You need to discover some of these things and react with empathy. But again, without good communication, you will not know what your partner likes.

The Future

Do you ever discuss the future with your partner? What do you think of the conversations? Are you in agreement about goals and visions? Some things affect the future of every couple. Finances, jobs, careers, money, children, etc., all determine how good your life together will be. And they are all about vision; what do you imagine life will be like on a day-to-day basis? What is your sense of purpose and goals together? Are you proactive in your relationship? Can you and your partner look ahead and actually point out the possibilities? What is important to both of you?

Sometimes people are afraid of talking about their dreams and goals with their partners because of rejection and criticism. If you cannot be open about your life, it might be time to reconsider your relationship. Can you tell your partner about the essential things in your life?

Compatibility: Individual Versus Couple Time

Compatibility is about expectations, visions, and needs regarding spending time, either together or apart. Does one of you expect that you will be sitting at the dinner table every evening while the other prefers to go to the movies? Is it okay for one of you to go and watch football matches while the other stays at home with the kids all weekend? Should you hang out with friends every Saturday or go shopping on some days? Again, the main issue in this matter is communication. You will need to spend time together and talk openly about it. How do you envision your future in terms of couple time and alone time?

Compatibility: Affection and Sex

Although some of these things change over time, it is important first to understand what you are walking into. Are you and your partner in agreement with each other about affection? What does your partner like? What do you prefer? Are you able to complement each other? Does one person feel sexually deprived while the other feels pressured? Differences in matters of affection and sex normally lead to a power struggle. The key here again is communication. You should be able to state what you want and listen to what your partner needs.

Compatibility: Work

Basically, this compatibility is not just about work but also the time spent at home. Does your partner work for 16 hours a day, make a lot of money, but is it never available for the kids? Do you want to handle that in the long term?

What About the Extended Family?

Extended family is known to bring complications to a relationship if boundaries are not set. It is essential to understand just how much of the extended family you will allow in your relationship. Is your mom allowed to come visiting any minute? Should we loan our siblings money now and then? Are we expected to attend all family events?

Technically, this is all about blending the family expectations and cultures-how. Do we ensure that our relationship withstands all the storms coming? Your mum can go over but not every minute. You can loan siblings money but with conditions, etc.

How About Your In-Laws?

Sometimes it can be challenging to get along with in-laws for different reasons. Maybe your mother-in-law seems to interfere with your life too much, or that sister-in-law is full of drama. How can you solve such conflicts?

The challenge of dealing with in-laws is that your partner's opinion might be biased because of the relationship. They might want to defend their relatives. So, you must be extra smart when dealing with this subject.

What Do You Consider Your Partner to Be?

It is easy to get a partner but hard to get a best friend or pillar of hope in the same person. Can you confidently say that your partner is your best friend? Does that person always have your back? Is your couple always willing to offer you the support required? Do you feel safe with them?

If your partner is just a person you are in a relationship with, you might not make some sacrifices for them. In fact, your intimacy will be limited. If 2 people can feel secure around each other, they will always find a way to resolve their conflicts.

When assessing your relationship, you need to be honest with yourself, dare to tell your partner what you are thinking, sort out the issues in your relationship, and know if you are headed anywhere or not. Define your visions, priorities, values, believes, etc., then check if they are compatible with your relationship.

Conclusion

As you continue with your relationship anxiety journey, know that you are going to have your own ups and downs. Sometimes, you might feel that you are in total control of your feelings. Other times, the anxiety is going to threaten to take over control. When you can find a balance, no matter what is going on, you are going to be a lot happier in your relationship. You should find solace in knowing that relationship anxiety is normal, and it is not your fault. Anxiety is a very powerful force that can be incredibly hard to control. Now that you understand what you can do about it, your healing journey can officially begin.

You can use this at any time that you feel you need additional support. When the anxiety is particularly bad, you can try different methods to combat it. There are also plenty of helpful hints throughout this that will remind you how to refocus your energy. When you become too focused and obsessive over one thought or idea, this is going to give your anxiety an invitation to come forward. You will be able to tell right away when you are not balanced. This is going to be your number one indicator that you must make a change to preserve your mental health and the health of your relationship.

Having doubts in any relationship is normal, no matter how long you have been together or how well you know each other. What is important is how you handle your doubts. If you keep them inside and allow them to torment you, this is going to impact the way that you feel about relationship anxiety. By having an honest conversation with your partner, you will have an outlet for your doubts while simultaneously receiving reassurance. Understand that it is not up to your partner to make you feel better though. You need to be able to calm yourself down and keep yourself in check.

Your past can trigger you and this is not your fault. If you have had horrible past relationship experiences, then it makes sense that you would carry these worries into your current relationship. What you need to remember is that not every relationship is going to mirror your past experiences. Even if you have been through plenty of hardship, know that not everyone is going to treat you this way. It can be incredibly difficult to separate the past from the present, but it is going to help you a lot. Therapy can become very beneficial for this purpose.

Even if you are not being triggered by your past, you can become triggered by certain things that your partner does. They might not be doing these things intentionally, but their actions could be causing you to experience anxiety. The most important thing for you to do is to tell them as soon as you realize what is happening. When you can work through these things together as a couple, you will both feel that you are on the same page. Understand that it might be you who needs to change, but if your partner is aware of what is bothering you about their behavior, they might be able to act more mindfully. You need to create a goal to not allow your anxiety to push you into a pattern of irrational behavior. This can happen very quickly, sometimes without you even realizing that it is happening. Irrational behavior is what leads to conflict. When you start fighting with your partner, this is going to lead to even more insecurity within the relationship. When you can recognize your own irrational behavior, you will be able to prevent or correct it. Understand that this is your anxious self-reacting and that you do not need to be this person all the time. Try your best to keep yourself grounded and in touch with reality. You can only focus on the things that you know are factual.

While this process sounds difficult, it can be a great way for you to reignite the spark that you have with your partner. When you can both get back in touch with the things that you love about one another, you will see that the chemistry remains. You do not need to let your anxiety get the best of you and get in the way of your relationship. All relationships are work, and you must be willing to put in the effort. When you become stagnant, your partner is going to feel this. Try your best to help the relationship bloom, and during your weaker moments, you should be able to lean on your partner as they put their effort in. All strong relationships have an equal hand from both partners.

Thank you very much for selecting this to help your relationship! Please remember to share all the ways that you were able to turn your marriage around. Relationship anxiety is very strong, but remember that you are stronger! As I expressed, I have also been through this same situation. It is incredibly difficult to manage at times, but there is a light at the end of the tunnel. You must not remain a victim of your own relationship anxiety. By breaking free of destructive thought patterns, you will be able to rediscover yourself and who you truly are. By allowing yourself to experience self-love, you will become a better partner by default. When times get tough, do not give up! Think about all the progress that you have made so far. From the instant that you started reading this, you became more educated on the topic of relationship anxiety; knowledge is power.

Hello reader!

If you enjoyed the book and found it useful help me let me know by writing an honest review, many thanks! ☺

Made in the USA
Las Vegas, NV
29 August 2023